The Way of the Dead Indians

Texas Press Sourcebooks in Anthropology, No. 13

The Way of the Dead Indians
GUAJIRO MYTHS AND SYMBOLS

By MICHEL PERRIN

Translated by Michael Fineberg in consultation with the author

 UNIVERSITY OF TEXAS PRESS, AUSTIN

Translation of *Le Chemin des Indiens morts: Mythes et symboles goajiro*, published by Editions Payot, Paris
Copyright © Payot, Paris 1976

Translation copyright © 1987 by the University of Texas Press
Printed in the United States of America

Requests for permission to reproduce material from
this English translation should be sent to:
  Permissions
  University of Texas Press
  Box 7819
  Austin, Texas 78713-7819

The preparation of this translation was made possible by grants
from the Translations Program of the National Endowment for the
Humanities, an independent federal agency, and from the Maison
des Sciences de l'Homme, Paris. The views, interpretations, and
conclusions contained herein should be understood to be solely
those of the author and should not be attributed to the National
Endowment for the Humanities or the Maison des Sciences de
l'Homme.

Library of Congress Cataloging-in-Publication Data
Perrin, Michel.
  The way of the dead Indians.
  Translation of: Le chemin des Indiens morts.
  Includes translations of Goajiro tales.
  Bibliography: p.
  Includes index.
  1. Goajiro Indians—Religion and mythology.
2. Goajiro Indians—Legends. 3. Indians of
South America—Colombia—Religion and mythology.
4. Indians of South America—Colombia—Legends.
5. Indians of South America—Venezuela—Religion and
mythology. 6. Indians of South America—Venezuela—
Legends. I. Title.
F2270.2.G6P4713 1987   299'.8   86-11299
ISBN 0-292-79032-5

nümüin tatushi wayu Iisho Jelipa Jayaliyu
nümüin tawala wayu Masakai Juse Uliyu

to my Guajiro grandfather "Isho" Felipe Jayariyu
to my Guajiro brother "Masakai" José Uliyu

Contents

Acknowledgments

All the ethnographic information and materials on which this book is based were collected during two periods I spent in Guajira, from 1969 to 1970 and in 1973. The second mission was financed by the Laboratoire d'Anthropologie Sociale of the Collège de France and the Centre National de la Recherche Scientifique (Paris).

Through his sense of human contact and his respect for others, Roberto Lizarralde developed my taste for ethnographic work; I owe him a great deal. My thanks go to him as well as to Jean Monod, who in 1969 encouraged me to continue studying the Guajiro.

I wish to express my deep gratitude to Professor Claude Lévi-Strauss, who took an interest in my work and was good enough to supervise it. My research benefited from his kind and constant support. I am also grateful to Yvette Perrin, and to Jean Claude Beaune and Michel Panoff, who read over the manuscript and gave me useful advice.

But it is of course to the Guajiro that I am chiefly indebted, for their friendliness, their patience, their trust. My goal will have been attained if, in this book that I dedicate to them, I have not betrayed them.

Note on the Transcription

To transcribe the Guajiro language, I have adopted a simplified system taking account as far as possible of the spelling and pronunciation of local Spanish, the second language of a growing number of Guajiro. Most of the orthographic signs used were proposed by Hildebrandt (1963). For an English reader, the major drawback to this system is the use of the letter *j* to convey the sound [*h*]. The sign ü signifies a central closed vowel situated between *i* and *u*, as in *mürülü* (domestic animal), and ' a mute occlusive glottal consonant, as in *ka'i* (sun). Long or germinated sounds are not shown.

The Guajiro names to which reference is sometimes made have in every case been reduced to their radicals. For example, for *spirit* (of the shaman) I have written *asheyu* (or *aseyu*) and not *taseyu* ("my spirit") or *washeyu* ("our spirit").

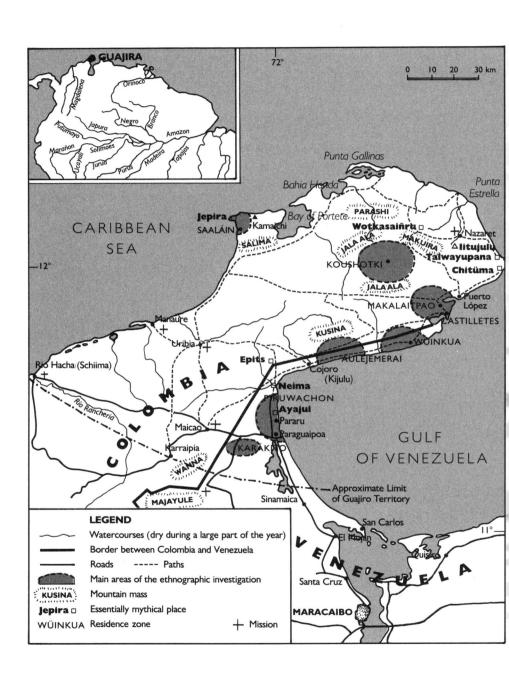

LEGEND

∿	Watercourses (dry during a large part of the year)
▬▬	Border between Colombia and Venezuela
▬▬	Roads ----- Paths
⬤	Main areas of the ethnographic investigation
KUSINA	Mountain mass
Jepira □	Essentially mythical place
WÜINKUA	Residence zone
✚	Mission

Map labels:

GUAJIRA

Orinoco
Magdalena
Putumayo
Japura
Negro
Branco
Marañon
Ucayali
Solimoes
Madeira
Tapajos
Juruá
Purus
Amazon

72°

0   10   20   30 km

Punta Gallinas

Bahia Honda

Punta Estrella

CARIBBEAN SEA

—12°

Jepira ▲
SAALÁIN ●   ● Kamaichi
SALIMA
Bay of Portete
PARASHI
Wotkasaiñru □
✚ Nazaret
JALA ALA
MAKUIRA
△ Iitujuiu
Talwayupana □
KOUSHOTKI ●
Chitüma □
JALA ALA
MAKALAITPAO
● Puerto López
ASTILLETES
KUSINA
● WÜINKUA
Manaure ✚
Uribia ✚
AULEJEMERAI
Río Hacha (Schiima)
✚
Río Ranchería
Epits □
Cojoro (Kijulu)
Neima ▲
RUWACHON
Ayajui □
□ Pararu
Maicao ✚
● Paraguaipoa
Karraipia
KARAKPO
WANNA
MAJAYULE ✚
Sinamaica
Approximate Limit of Guajiro Territory

C O L O M B I A

GULF OF VENEZUELA

11°

San Carlos
El Moján
Quisiro
Santa Cruz
V E N E Z U E L A
MARACAIBO

Introduction

In America today, when an old man dies, a library goes up in flames.

So it is in the America of the Guajiro Indians,[1] a people of distant Arawak origins living in a semidesert peninsula that one day in the last century, without their being consulted, was shared between Venezuela and Colombia.[2] Today there are over one hundred thousand of them, living in increasingly close contact with what usually goes by the name of "civilization," present in all the market towns that dot the southern part of the peninsula—Rio Hacha, Uribia, and Maicao in Colombia, Paraguaipoa in Venezuela. This so-called civilization rules supreme a hundred or so miles away in Maracaibo, a sprawling oil metropolis and regional capital with more than six hundred thousand inhabitants that put forth its tentacular highways, trucks, and gadgets and lured a large number of Guajiro men, wore them out in thankless, temporary jobs, then rejected or destroyed them, and now continues inexorably to drain the lifeblood from an entire people.

This process, however, did not begin either violently or suddenly for the Guajiro. The beginning of the colonial period was marked by the free and gradual assimilation of stock breeding, now the dominant form of economic activity. The Indians then became involved in various activities resulting from "civilization," such as the slave trade and pearl fishing. Finally, the West purely and simply established itself in Indian territory, through the foundation of a Christian mission—several times frustrated but still present today; the building and then improvement of access and transit roads; and later the establishment of centers for Indian affairs, responsible for bringing "progress and civilization" to the Guajiro.

Today the industrial world is more forcefully present than ever. The process of acculturation that started more than four centuries ago is speeding up notably. Radically disorganized, this people is once again being brought under the yoke of history. And perhaps it will not have the means of achieving a new balance, of adapting while remaining true to itself. It will then be doomed, like so many others, to vanish in the back streets of the big cities or to fuel the hopes of industrial agriculture.

Guajiro society, however, continues to live, tragically divided but present—despite the fact that its young people are irresistibly drawn along the newly tarmacked highways that lead to Ziruma or Los Olivos, the Indian shantytown of Maracaibo; despite the disarray of the elders, who see the world of yesteryear becoming increasingly remote; despite the appearance of an uncontrollable and cruel form of delinquency in places where two civilizations, theirs and ours, come into direct confrontation and negate one another in a cultural wilderness steeped in ashes and blood.

Today the Guajiro still exist.

Women riding mules in long caravans outlined against a white sky, across a vast expanse of barren mountains or arid plains dotted with xerophilous bushes and torch cacti, beneath the torrid breath of a continual east wind. Haunting, lusterless faces, painted to the eyes in red, black, or ocher; deeply lined faces of old women bent forward against the muted evening light. Young women busy at their looms seated beneath the sun roof at the edge of the desert; their bodies extended by dresses that trail out on the ground as, swaying in the wind, they move with elegance over an open plain covered in short grasses and cacti. Herdsmen pattering behind their herds; a tottering line of men befuddled by alcohol; the hard, fixed gaze of one who does not know you . . . Uncomfortable but merry journeys in old, gaudily painted trucks in which men and women laugh, joke, tell stories, and ask questions, squeezed together for hours on hard planks laid out over lowing cattle or among multicolored bundles . . .

Twice a year, during the rainy season, the landscape undergoes a metamorphosis, without losing any of its larger-than-life qualities. The colorless sky, shimmering in the heat, gives way to a sky covered by turbulent clouds, a deep, dark, immense sky shattered by violent storms. The torch cacti are reflected in a greenish water. The wind drops. Men become slower in their movements. Life gathers to a point. Children lightheartedly play in ponds. With solemn gestures couples sow their gardens. At nightfall, beneath the fumes of odoriferous plants that for a moment hold at bay the swarms of mosquitoes, the circle of women contracts. Insects, batrachians, and mollusks perform a hypnotic ballet.

At first, it seemed to the foreigner that a few images would suffice to sum up centuries of traditions and customs—short-lived illusion! Upon this fascinating world he had been projecting his own symbols, his own values.

And so, for days and days on end, he listened to the words of those who still know. Reclining in their hammocks in the evening, a time that lends itself to the excavation of memories, men and women repeated the words of their ancestors. Day after day they became engrossed in painting a picture of the world they had created, the heritage they had received from their forebears, which, to their sorrow, they dimly felt was in the process of disappearing. The originality of that world was immediately apparent in every one of those stories, which were the result of centuries of community life and shared thoughts.

Brief Ethnographic Note

The Guajiro form one of the largest Indian ethnic groups in the lowlands of South America. They live on the Guajira peninsula, which juts out into the Caribbean Sea at the northernmost tip of the continent. It is a region of "shrubland," for the most part covered with xerophilous vegetation interspersed here and there with desert areas. Nine months out of twelve, drought prevails.

The Guajiro are distributed between Venezuela and Colombia. Although nine-tenths of their territory is in Colombia, about a quarter of them live in Venezuela. More than ten thousand Guajiro now live in the suburbs of the city of Maracaibo.[3]

The Guajiro are stock breeders. Cattle possess the greatest value for them, but because of severe ecological constraints they cannot be raised everywhere. Livestock therefore consists mainly of sheep and goats; from these the Guajiro derive the major part of their resources, eating their meat and drinking their milk. Livestock—including horses and mules, which enjoy great prestige—is the most important element in marriage settlements and serves for the payment of fines and compensations of every kind. Moreover, it provides the Guajiro with the major part of their monetary revenue, for at regular intervals the Indians go off to sell a few animals in the outlying markets of Rio Hacha, Uribia, and Maicao in Colombia and Paraguaipoa in Venezuela (Photographs 20–22). These weekly markets have come to assume great importance in the economic life of the Guajiro. With the money obtained from the sale of their livestock and a few of their craft products, mainly beautifully made hammocks and bags woven by the women, the Guajiro buy basic foodstuffs—sugar, salt, coffee, bananas—and manufactured goods—metal tools, firearms, matches, and so on.

Hunting, and in the coastal region fishing, have become secondary economic activities; only a minute number of Guajiro live exclusively from them. But great prestige still attaches to these practices, which are invested with high symbolic value. The game they hunt consists mainly of different varieties of deer, peccaries, rabbits,[4] and a few species of birds. For religious and medical reasons, however, the Guajiro also hunt other animals to which they attribute a number of diseases and misfortunes.

Each Guajiro family keeps a garden where, as soon as the first rains fall, corn, cassava, various kinds of beans, muskmelon, and watermelon are planted. But gardening activities are short-lived; for at most two or three months they augment each family's food resources. The Guajiro also gather wild fruits. Nowadays this is an activity engaged in during the dry season by those who live far from the borders of the Indian territory, and an occasional activity or one reserved for the poor in areas close to the markets where supplies can be obtained periodically.

The Guajiro live in scattered settlements. The nuclear family's living area consists of a small house where the hammocks are hung up at night, a space enclosed by a fence of cacti or branches serving as the kitchen, a sun roof—a flat roof resting on posts—beneath which the day's activities take place, and, further on, one or two corrals for the sheep and goats. The residential unit is constituted by a few dozen similar dwellings scattered over an area of a hundred acres or more.[5] Each of these units has its own name, but strictly speaking there is no Guajiro "village."

Guajiro society is organized in matrilineal, nonexogamous clans, each of them associated with a totemic animal. There are about thirty clans, greatly varying in size. At the present time they are confined to no particular place but are scattered throughout the territory.[6] Some clans are reputed to be poor—for example, the Wouliyu clan, associated with the partridge—and others rich and politically influential—for example, the Uliana clan, associated with the jaguar. In theory, then, an individual's social identity and status are defined by membership in a particular clan. In reality, however, the clans have lost their sociological and political importance; their role in this respect has been assumed by smaller matrilineal units.[7]

The Guajiro conform theoretically to a rule of matrilocal residence: a young couple lives provisionally in the wife's mother's house before building another dwelling in a place close to the first. The woman thus remains attached to her matrilineage while the man is usually removed from his. But there is more to it than this. As a result of polygyny, to which a great deal of prestige is attached and which is practiced by about one Guajiro man in five, the polygamous male becomes a perpetual wanderer as his time has to be shared out among wives who may live at great distances from one another.[8]

Guajiro girls undergo an arduous rite of passage. As soon as menstruation begins, they must live in seclusion for a period ranging from a few months to several years, according to their social rank. Boys do not undergo either a rite of passage or any form of initiation. Guajiro children are educated by their mothers in their early years. Subsequently, and for some time, a boy is generally placed under the authority of the uterine uncle of whom he will later be one of the heirs, while a girl goes off to live with an aunt or a close maternal kinswoman.

PART ONE

Süküjala Alaülayu:
Tales of the Elders

Note on the Translation of the Myths

The words of the storytellers were first transcribed in the vernacular from recordings on magnetic tape, then translated into Spanish with the help of several young bilingual Guajiro. All texts included in this work respect the original documents as far as possible but do not always represent a literal translation of them. To facilitate understanding, sentence order has sometimes been modified and the number of involuntary repetitions and references to previous events has been reduced.

The presentation of the texts in the form of free verse is not the result of striving after facile effects. The Guajiro have a style of narration characterized by short sentences, which creates a rhythm different from that of our written prose. Rendered as free verse, the texts have to be read in much the same way as they are recited by the Indians.

Those Guajiro terms that have no close English equivalents have been left in the vernacular. Similarly, a few English words have been printed in italics: these are words that correspond only in part to Guajiro notions or are so emotionally charged for us that they are in danger of being interpreted in too subjective or culture-specific a way. Their significance will be pinpointed in the analysis that follows.

You have set down well what we recounted to you.
That is good.
Thus our name will be in a book
and will not be lost for ever.
Later our young men in trousers,
unhearing today,
will perhaps come and seek here
what the elders knew in former times.

(Iisho, Jelipa Jayaliyu)

Six years ago, in 1969, an old man for the first time welcomed me, a foreigner eager to discover, through his myths and traditional tales, a spiritual universe that until then had been described only from the outside and all too often had been reduced to caricature.

Felipe Fernández—known as Iisho—an influential member of the Jayaliyu clan (see Photograph 1), was on the occasion of my first stay at once my host, guide, informant, contact man, fall guy, and friend. This dynamic man, the father of more than fifty children by seven wives, was about seventy years old, and so his time was his own except when he was called upon to settle disputes in his capacity as *ma'ünai* or mediator. Formerly the owner of a large herd, he said that he had been a victim of the protracted drought that prevailed during the fifties and destroyed most of his livestock, thus irremediably reducing his political power. In reality, this "mortal blow" stemmed from a more deep-seated phenomenon: the gradual shift from a traditional form of power, distributed in accordance with the pattern of clans and lineages, to a new form of power, based on money and social mobility, contended for by the mestizos of the border zones.

Since that time Iisho has lived on his prestige and memories. Thrilled by the idea that his name would not be forgotten if it appeared in a book, aware of the importance for *us*, but also for his own people, of preserving the knowledge of the elders, convinced that he would gain prestige in the company of a foreigner, he cooperated unstintingly. This book is also his.

The following tales have been faithfully reproduced without commentary, nor do they include any material that did not originate with the Guajiro Indians themselves—both out of respect for that people and so that those who wish to read them through from beginning to end can freely ask their own questions. Let them have, if only for a while, the illusion of being in the position of both the ethnographer who, out there, has no choice but to listen, to question, and to see, and of the ethnologist who, confronted by these messages from another world, endeavors to understand and to communicate in his own language what has been revealed.

It is clear, however, that the selection, arrangement, and presentation of these texts, linked by a fictional narrator, are the fruit of long contact with the Guajiro and thoughtful inquiry into their world. The way in which they have been arranged is to some extent a reflection of the analysis developed in the second part of the book. While not making that analysis unnecessary, this arrangement is intended to lead readers gradually into the Guajiro universe of death and the beyond, with the desire that such a protracted face-to-face encounter may help them better to combat that claim to universality which we "Westerners" carry before us like a screen, determining in advance our perceptions, our associations, our judgments, and our analyses.

sonokalaka e atüjain
e matüjain nojotsü,
wonokaliaka süma ekai atüjain.

Those who know believe in it.
Those who know nothing do not believe in it.
We who know, we believe in it.

(An old shaman)

GUAJIRO DEATH

To each of us is attached a *soul*.[1]
It is like a bit of white cotton fluff,
like smoke.
But no one can see it.

5 Everywhere our soul follows us
like our shadow.
Some even say that the shadow is the form of the *soul*
and to the *soul* they give the name of shadow.

Our *soul* leaves us only when we sleep
10 or when we are sick,
when we have been pierced by the arrow of a *wanülü*.

Everything that happens in our *dreams*
is what happens to our *soul*.
If a Guajiro starts dreaming that he is elsewhere,
15 near a well or in a house,
or if he sees birds,
this means that his *soul* has left his *heart*,
na'in wayu ajuitüsü sulu na'in,
by way of his mouth
20 to fly away over yonder.
But his *heart* continues to work.

And yet it's our *soul* that makes us die.
He who dreams that he is dead never wakes up again.
His *soul* has left him forever.
25 He is still alive,
he who dreams that a knife has been stuck in his chest,
but his *soul* is already wounded.
Sickness is there.
Death is near.

30 When a Guajiro is sick,
it's as though his *soul* were a prisoner in Dream's abode.

It's there that the *spirit*[2] of the shaman
can find it and bring it back to the sick man.
But if he doesn't find it,
35   if it is hidden,
if it has gone back somewhere,
the Guajiro dies.
His *soul* has crossed the way,
the way of the dead Indians:
40   *spüna wayu ouktüsü*,[3]
the Milky Way.
It heads for the sea,
to go to the house where already are gathered
sisters, mothers, maternal uncles, brothers . . .

45   And the dying man breathes his last words:
"I'm going off now, I'm going off.
I'm going to die.
I'm going off and will never be back."
But already his *soul* has left and will never be back.
50   It has taken its mount.
It has loaded it with baggage and hammocks.
It has gone to its homeland,
over there, in Jepira, the land of the *yolujas*.
When they die, the Guajiro become *yolujas*.
55   They go to Jepira, by the Milky Way,
the way of the dead Indians.
There is where their houses are.

It is the *souls* of the dead who come back to earth
by way of our dreams.
60   They are the ones that are met by our *souls*
when we dream of the dead.
Here sometimes their shadows are seen.
They are the *yolujas*,
shadows of the dead on earth.

65   When we die, then, our *soul* is not lost.
Only our bones are lost.
Our bones and our skin.
Our *soul* goes off, that is all.
What leaves is like our shadow,
70   or like our silhouette, blurred, hazy . . .

But we die twice,
once here
and once in Jepira.

(Recounted by Makaerü Jitnu, Setuma Pushaina, Semaria Apshana, Ramansita Uliyu, and "Masakai" Uliyu.)

THE JOURNEY TO THE BEYOND: A GUAJIRO EURYDICE

Eshi wane wayu chi ouktüsü nierüin
75 *nialajaka weinshi süchirua . . .*
A Guajiro Indian wept so long,
so long for his dead wife
that she took pity on him.

One night she came to him,
80 in a dream.
She looked human.
She seemed to be alive.

She came toward him.
"My wife! My wife! Stop!
85 I am here! Don't leave me!"
cried the Guajiro, rising to his feet.
She did not answer.
Going past him, she quickened her step.

The Guajiro gave chase to her.
90 He ran,
but he couldn't catch up with her.
He was close,
but he couldn't seize hold of her.

When the next day dawned she spoke to him.
95 "Why are you chasing me?
I am lost, I have come to the end.
I am a shade in the land of darkness.
But come with me if such is your wish!
Come with me since you weep."

100 She took him on her shoulders
and they went off far away,
toward the center of the sea,
in the direction of Jepira,
the realm of the dead Guajiro.

105 She moved upon the water
very fast,
like a pelican.
Soon they reached the other shore.

"Follow me! Hurry up!
110 I am thirsty!" she said.
The Guajiro hastened on.

They then met with Bittern,
the keeper of the water.
The water drunk by the *yolujas* is in enclosed ground.
115 Bittern bars the way.

Bittern was standing there.
"You must stop here!"
said the woman to her husband.
The thirsty Guajiro gazed at the water.
120 He hurried toward it.
Bittern made him drink first.
Then the woman drank.

They continued on their way.

"That's what I dreamt of,"
125 said the Guajiro further on, seeing a door.
The door opened by itself.
The Guajiro rushed forward to be the first one through.
His wife ran up to try to stop him.
"Stay behind me!" she shouted.
130 But he was already halfway through.

They went on walking.

At dawn
they found themselves by a mountain.
Here was where the woman lived.
135 Before reaching the summit,
they passed over shifting, muddy ground,
over a land in which one sinks:
wanee mma mokomokosü.

Drunken talk could be heard.
140 A bull bellowed, goats bleated:
they had been eaten at a dead man's burial.
And on dead horses drunken *yolujas* galloped.
When they arrived,
when the sun had risen,
145 the long-dead hailed the Guajiro.
"Brother-in-law!" said one.
"How are you, friend?" asked another.
"Cousin!" exclaimed a third.
They were all *yolujas.*

150   The Guajiro alone still looked like a living man.

There they ate muskmelon and watermelon.
Each morning
a pot with cooked food awaited him.

Thus, for many days, he stayed with her.

155   At night,
when his wife wished to lie with him,
she hung up the hammock.
But when he drew near her,
ready to take her,
160   she vanished.
He fell flat on the floor,
and he saw her again standing beside him.
She did not want to let him couple with her.
For a long time she behaved in this way.

165   "They have come to take me dancing,
but you stay here!" she said to him one day.
A *yonna* dance had been organized.
All the *yolujas* were invited.
"I'm coming with you!" said the Guajiro.
170   He went to follow her.
"They'll do things to me there you wouldn't like to see!"

The place where the ball was being held was lit up.
A large number of people dressed in red were dancing.
Everything appeared red.
175   Someone was playing a drum.

The dancers stopped to rest.
Some went off toward a house.
Stretched out on hammocks, they could take their ease.

"Wait for me here!" said the woman.
180   But the Guajiro insisted on following her.
Together they went on to another house.
"Now you stay here! I'll bring you food!"

This time the Guajiro let her go.

Immediately afterward,
185   some young men came up to her.
They embraced her.
They kissed her on the mouth.

The Guajiro had moved forward to get a better view.

He was very shocked.
190 He turned round and went back toward the house.

The woman changed her dress.
and started to dance again.
Her husband didn't take his eyes off her.

Toward noon,
195 she brought him a large muskmelon.
"Eat with me," he said.
"No! I don't want anything, I've already eaten."
He insisted.
She shared his meal with him in the house.
200 Then she went off and started dancing again.

The Guajiro was sitting down,
but no one came near him.

When night fell
he rushed off to the ball.
205 But when he wanted to dance everyone fled
because he was awake,
because he was alive.

His wife danced all night long.
He searched for her
210 but couldn't find her.
Women were lying around,
legs wide apart.
All night long they remained separated.

At dawn,
215 the Guajiro sighted a table
laden with all kinds of cooked foods.
It seemed to him they had got there by themselves,
without anyone preparing them.

He was shown the table,
220 he was told to help himself.
But he preferred to eat alone,
alone in his house.
His wife, however, made her way to the table.

When the sun set,
225 still no one had come near him.

Then he saw a man come up,
he who had been the first to lie with his wife,
once only, before her marriage.

The man coupled with her
230 while other men,
those who'd had her next,
entered her from all sides,
one here, one there,
one through an ear,
235 one through her nose . . .

The Guajiro was very upset.
He left at dawn.

But the path by which they'd come forked.
The Guajiro went the wrong way.
240 He chose the way that led to Juya, to Rain.[4]
Lost,
throughout one cycle of the moon,
he walked.

He gathered gourds and dates,
245 malpighia and *koushot* berries.
They were there for him,
and he could eat his fill.

Each morning,
Juya's milch cows came toward him.
250 In the evening, on their way back,
they passed by him again.
One of them was old,
weighed down with milk,
and straggled along behind.

255 "Where can they be coming from?"
the Guajiro wondered.
One day
he clutched hold of the old cow's tail,
and thus it was that he arrived in Juya's domain.

260 Juya watched him draw near.
"Here's my grandson!"
he said, embracing him.
"How did you get here?"
"I walked."
265 "Sit down on my bench."[5]
"But it's a boa,"
said the Guajiro to himself, seized with panic.
"Come on! Sit down!"

"If I'm to die, then I'll die."
270   The Guajiro sat down reluctantly.
At once the bench curled up.

"Go and fetch me a watermelon
for my grandson to eat!"
Juya then ordered.
275   The Guajiro cut up the fruit.
A single slice was enough to fill him up.

"There's a lot of game here:
partridges, rabbits, brockets, deer . . .
First go and get some brockets
280   as I want to eat some,"
said Juya to him.
The man set off in search of a brocket.
He met a *kusina* Indian[6]
who was holding an arrow in his hand
285   and carrying a crown made of cassia bark,
topped with cock feathers.
"I say, where are you going?" he asked the Guajiro.
"Good morning,
I'm searching for brockets," said the Guajiro.
290   "Search! Search!"
The Guajiro did not meet a single brocket.
Weary, he came back.
"Well, what did you find?" Juya asked him.
"A man carrying an arrow and a cassia crown."
295   "That's it! Pierce him with an arrow!"
The Guajiro went off again and shot his arrows.
He came back laden with brockets.

"I want to eat venison!
Go get me a deer!" said Juya.
300   The Guajiro met a rich Indian.
He was wearing a red belt, a robe, and a hat.[7]
"Where are you going?" the rich man asked him.
"I'm searching for deer!"
"Search! Search!"
305   The Guajiro found nothing.
He came back when he was weary.
"Well?" said Juya.
"I met only a rich Indian."
"That's it! Shoot him!"
310   The Guajiro went off again and shot at the Indian.
He brought back a deer.

"Now go and fetch me some rabbits!"
"I didn't see any rabbits,
I saw people playing *oulakawa*
315   with *walerü* creepers."⁸
"That's it! Go hunt them!" said Juya.
The Guajiro went and shot arrows at them.
They at once took the form of mere rabbits.

"I have all kinds of cultivated plants here:
320   watermelons, muskmelons, sweet corn, gourds . . .
What do you want to eat?"
Juya now asked him.
"I'd like to eat some watermelon."
"Go and get some!"
325   The Guajiro went off.
"I am a friend of Juya!" said a watermelon.
The watermelons spoke,
they had human form.
"Hello," replied the Guajiro.
330   "What are you looking for?"
"I'm looking for watermelons!"
"Well, go on looking!"
The Guajiro came back.
He had found nothing.
335   "What did you see?" Juya asked him.
"I saw black-skinned people with their children."
"That's it! They're the ones!
You have to get near them!"
The Guajiro went off again.
340   He brought back a ripe, raw, juicy watermelon.
"Is this it?"
he asked on his return.
"Yes, you are to eat it this very day,
all of it!" said Juya.

345   "What do you want now?"
"I want to eat some gourd!"
"Go and get some!"
The Guajiro met some people with fat bellies, with huge
    bellies.
"Where are you going?" they asked him.
350   "I'm going to look for gourds!"
"Well, go on then!"
The Guajiro found nothing.
He came back when he felt tired.

"Well?" said Juya.
355   "There aren't any!"
"What did you see?"
"Men with fat bellies!"
"That's it! Go get them!"
"What will he do now?" Juya wondered.
360   The Guajiro went off again.
"Is this right?"
he said on his return.
"Yes, that's right!"
He cut the gourd in two,
365   but he took very little.

"What do you want now?"
"I want to eat some corn!"
"Go and get some!"
"How many people with hairy pubes will he see?"
370   Juya wondered.
"What did you see?"
he asked when the Guajiro came back.
"I saw people with very hairy pubes!"
"They are the ones! Go back to them!"
375   The Guajiro brought back corn.

"How about melons? Do you have any?"
"There are some down there," said Juya.
"I want to eat some!"
"What will he do with the little *alijunas*?"⁹
380   Juya wondered.
The Guajiro looked everywhere,
but he saw only *alijunas*, white people.
When he felt tired he turned back.
"I saw only *alijunas*."
385   "That's it! Go get them!"
The Guajiro came back with melons.

Juya then said:
"You'll stay here, grandson,
I'm going off now,
390   but you're not to budge!
Nothing will happen to you.
But take care!
Don't go walking near my wife.
Pülasü tia:
395   She has supernatural powers.
Her house is close by here

in this direction.
In front there's a large sun roof.
Don't go near,
400   that's where she lives."
His wife was Pulowi.
Püloi nierüin Juya, münüshi:
Pulowi is Juya's wife, the Guajiro say.

Juya went off.
405   Rain was to fall, somewhere on the earth.
The Guajiro watched him leave with his bottles.
Juya always carries bottles with him
so that he can put men's blood in them.
The blood isn't lost.
410   He takes it back to Pulowi for her to drink.
Pulowi never eats with him.
She feeds on the blood of Indians.

No one was there any longer.
The Guajiro started walking.
415   "What does his wife look like,
the woman with supernatural powers?"
he wondered.
He wanted to go and see.

The Guajiro looked through the window.
420   He then saw Juya's wife
without a loincloth,
her legs wide apart.
When his eyes lighted on her
she exploded:
425   *"Ouu . . . ooolojolon!"*
The Guajiro was hurled to the ground
face down.
He dropped dead,
to the west of the sunroof.

430   Juya had heard everything.
"Oh! That man did not heed my advice."
He decided to return home.

When Juya arrived
the Guajiro had long been stretched out on the ground.
435   His belly was already swollen.
Juya seized hold of him and set him back on his feet.
"Woe to the man who pays no heed!
Why did you do that?

Because of you I'll be blamed!" said Juya.
440   "Sleep now! Sleep!" he said.
And he went off to see Pulowi.

"What has happened to my grandson?
Why is he dead?"
Juya asked Pulowi.
445   "He is dead because he looked,"
replied his wife.
"Why did you go and get that man?
I should eat him,
like everything you collect."
450   "Eat him if you want."

From anger Juya had uttered these words.
"I'll be able to divide him in two.
Tomorrow I'll eat half,"
Pulowi then said.

455   But over there lived Aleket—Spider—
a little old lady with white hair.
She had heard everything
and she went and told the Guajiro.
"Pulowi is going to eat you tomorrow!
460   Because of you they have quarrelled
and Juya has given you up to her.
But if you wanted to get away
I could guide you.
We would set off in the night.
465   At dawn we would be near your home.
I know where you are from
for I am close to Juya.
I know the name of the place where you live."
"I'll do what you propose,"
470   said the Guajiro.

During the night
he went to see Spider.
"Climb up behind," she said to him.
She started coming down.
475   She made a ball of fine thread.
Unwinding the thread,
secreting her line,
she "carried him off" to the place he had started from,
close to his house.

480 Before letting him go
    Spider said to him:
    "When you get home
    your mother and your sister will be frightened.
    They will want to weep for you.[10]
485 Don't let them.
    For if they weep
    you will die.
    Nor should you speak of what you have seen.
    If you keep the secret,
490 you'll be able to go walking a long time yet.
    If not, you'll die."

    The Guajiro's hair had grown;
    it reached far down.
    His beard was long;
495 it was a long time since he had shaved.
    "Where have you come from?"
    his mother and sister asked him.
    "If I tell you what I have done
    I'll die," said the Guajiro.
500 He told them nothing.
    His sister wept.
    "Do not weep for me," he ordered.
    When he was with them,
    he took care to say nothing.

505 But one day he told them where he had been.
    When he had finished his story,
    he died.

    He went straight to Jepira,
    the land of the *yolujas.*

(Recounted by Luka Iipuana on December 23, 1969, then on August 1, 1973. This man, some fifty years old, lives by fishing and stock raising at Wüinkua, in Venezuelan Guajira.)

510 Do you understand, *alijuna,* foreigner?
    If he had not sought to see Pulowi,
    the Guajiro would have stayed over there,
    in Juya's domain.
    But Juya and Pulowi are enemies,
515 though husband and wife.
    Sometimes they are great enemies.

Do you know the story of the Pulowi of Ayajui?
Ayajui[11] is that big dune near to the sea,
to the east of Paraguaipoa.
520   At the top there is a small pool of stagnant, reddish water.
It never dries up,
even in the hottest summers.
Many Guajiro died because they touched that water,
or simply because they went near it.
525   As soon as they got back home,
they started to swell.
They died soon after.
Even now, the land of Ayajui is *pulowi*.
You yourself, *alijuna*, foreigner,
530   if you do not want to die,
do not go walking alone on the top of Ayajui.
You do not have supernatural powers,
you would be helpless . . .

THE PULOWI OF AYAJUI AND THE DAUGHTERS OF JUYA

Nia chi Juyakai kerüinshi wayu wüinpümüin . . .
535   Juya had a wife in Upper Guajira.[12]
She was a *pülainrü* Indian,
a pretentious woman who disparaged men.
She always remained secluded,
but nonetheless Juya had given her two daughters.

540   "These girls can be had by anyone!"
Every day, every day,
the scandalmongers spread such tales
and refused to see them.

This caused the girls much suffering.
545   Soon they could not bear it anymore.
They decided to leave, at the risk of losing their way.

"Our father's lightning flash is over yonder.
He knows that here he has children.
It would be best to go and join him.
550   We'll see how he greets us,"
said the younger daughter.
The older daughter acquiesced.
Their father did not live far away.

The girls were rich.

555   They ordered their servant to accompany them.
"Round up three good mules,
two for us and one for you,"
they told him.

They set out,
560   guided by their father's lightning flash.
From Kajuo to Neima all went well.
At Neima the girls decided to ride the same mule.
"If we are lucky,
our father will look after us
565   and we'll stay over there.
Otherwise we'll come back,"
they said to their servant before dismissing him.

He returned along the seashore
with the two other mules.

570   On the hindquarters of their mount,
the girls secured their woven bag.
Along the shore they continued on their way.
"If now we meet up with something harmful,
we're lost," they said.

575   Their mule was on the look-out.
It trotted along warily.
Suddenly,
before Ayajui mountain,
it came to a halt.

580   "Over there, there's a man!"
The girls had sighted a *parauja*,[13] a fisherman.
"Is it really a man?"
asked the elder.
(She knew that Ayajui was *pulowi*,
585   that she could assume the form of an Indian.)

When they had drawn near
they had to bow their heads.[14]
Immediately afterward
the man vanished.
590   "He's certainly not a Guajiro:
let's change route and avoid him," said the younger.

The fisherman broke wind loudly.
Suddenly he changed into a snake.
The girls foundered.
595   Anna'uy,[15]

the snake who lives in Ayajui's entrails,
was swallowing them down.

In the storm
the girls flung down a small calabash.
600   The calabash fought with the snake,
but it broke
and the snake went on swallowing them.

Then Pachanoi, Dragonfly,
likewise a son of Juya,
605   passed that way
in the form of a Guajiro.
"Help! Help!
We can't get away.
Bear our name to our father,
610   tell him Pulowi has swallowed his daughters and their mule!"
they just had time to shout.

Pulowi first swallowed the elder,
then the younger.

The old Dragonfly had heard all their words
615   and he set off to see Juya.

"Where have you come from, my child?"
"I have come to see you
because your Guajiro daughters have been swallowed by
    Pulowi."
Juya remembered the girls.
620   "They are my daughters!
I do not usually forget," he said,
and he wept.

He immediately suspected Ayajui.
He sent for Iiwa and Oummala.[16]
625   "Help me! My daughters have vanished,
Pulowi has swallowed them.
Let's see how long she can stand up to us!"
They left at once.

Juya began to crackle
630   accompanied by Iiwa and Oummala.
Juya was the fastest.
They shattered Ayajui,
they broke him into several pieces.

The girls were in the bowels of the earth

635 with their mount,
dying of hunger.
They were able to get them out.
But Pulowi was done for.

"Father, we came to visit you
640 because scandalmongers were making trouble for us.
They said that we fornicated with everyone."
"I am glad that you got away,"
Juya said to them.
They left with him and went very far,
645 all the way to his house.

Ale'eja joo'o juyain mapa nümaanamüin:
Later the girls came back in the form of rains.

In earlier days
Ayajui was a very big mountain.
650 But she did wrong and had to pay for it.
Her pieces are now scattered
through the length and breadth of Guajira.
They are the dunes along the coast.

The blood that can be seen today
655 to the east of Ayajui hill
in a hole in the earth
is the blood of the snake Anna'uy.

(Story told by Mapua Uraliyu, alias Eugenio Fernández, on July 6,
1969. This stock breeder lived in Pararu, near to Ayajui dune. He died
in 1972, aged about seventy.)

Do you know other *pulowis, alijuna?*
There are many of them in Guajira.
660 Do you know the *pulowi* of Ishiwo,
that of Kalanapai, that of Komocho'jülü,
that of Kalarapana?
And that of Yaulama in Upper Guajira?
I lived near there.
665 I know her well . . .

THE PULOWI OF YAULAMA

Yaulama is a mountain where there is a *pulowi.*
Esü wuchi pülasü:
it is a *magic* mountain.

At the top are said to be seas,
670   many animals, birds and fierce snakes.
All kinds of plants grow there
but it is dangerous to pick them.

When during the dry season,
at noon,
675   the Guajiro go on that mountain
to steal the huge gourds that ripen there
or to seek, for the sake of wealth, maguey fibers,
or powerful and dangerous plants, like the roucou,
or the plants from which they make *wunu'u lania*—
680   amulets that fetch high prices—
the seas fill up,
the wind begins to blow.
They are attacked by fierce hummingbirds
and poisonous snakes.
685   Some never come back.
If they go too close to the *pulowi,*
men are turned into winds.
They are eaten
or they start swelling.

(Story told by Kaliwajut Epieyu, alias María, on September 22, 1969.
Aged about eighty, she lives at Aulejemerai, in Venezuelan Guajira.)

690   All the *pulowis* are the wives of Juya,
and Juya has countless wives.

Have you heard of those girls called Kulamia or Julamia?
They are *pülainrü* girls
—pretentious girls,
695   always living secluded lives,
spurning all the men who want to be their husbands—
Juya and Epeyüi, the jaguar with supernatural powers,
are the only men the Kulamia cannot resist.
All the human wives of Juya are *pülainrü* girls.
700   The daughters of Juya, swallowed by Pulowi at Ayajui,
were the daughters of a *pülainrü* Indian woman.

Juya is the husband of the *pulowis* around here
and the husband of the *pulowis* of the sea.
And they sometimes are enemies of one another:
705   In olden times,
Pulowi of the sea was much richer than Pulowi of the land.
She possessed *tu'umas.*

Tu'umas are the most precious of Guajiro jewels.
They are made of marine stone.
710 They are given to the family of one's future wife.
They serve to pay the shaman who has healed.[17]
Pulowi of the land possessed rabbits and deer,
but she had neither *tu'umas* nor gold
nor all the other precious things that were found in the sea.

715 But nowadays
tu'umas are also to be found on land.
Listen to what the elders relate:

PULOWI OF THE SEA AND PULOWI OF THE LAND

*Tü Pülouikat anoitpajakat, kaja tü palairakakat
nierüinja Juyaaya . . .*
720 The Pulowi of the deep sea
and the Pulowi who dwells on land
are both the wives of Juya.

Pulowi of the deep sea is the richer.
For *livestock* she has turtles, fishes,
725 and all the other animals of the sea.
She possesses vast quantities of *tu'umas*,
and jewels of all kinds.

Pulowi of the land is poor.
For livestock she has but deer, brockets, foxes,
730 and a few other animals.

One day, from Pulowi of the sea,
she decided to steal a bag of *tu'umas*.

"Why don't you send me along?"
said the *si'a* bird, the troopial.
735 "*Pülashi pia?* Do you have supernatural powers
that you think you can bring me back her jewels?"

"Yes, like her I am *pülashi*,"
the little *si'a* bird replied to Pulowi of the land.
"Then go,
740 and come back with the finest jewels.
I shall say that you are *pülashi*
only when from Pulowi of the land, my husband's other wife,
you have brought me a bag of the finest jewels."

The *si'a* bird went a long way off,

745 as far as the shore,
then he came to Pulowi who dwells in the sea,
in a very big house
which she shares with her children,
the daughters of Juya.

750 "*Antshi pia wayu!* There you are, Guajiro!
I've never seen you before. Where do you come from?
How did you get all the way here?
What do you seek,
Indian from elsewhere, far away from here?"
755 Pulowi asked him.
"I like exploring the world
and I want to know you."

"So you want to stay here?
Go and sling a hammock for this Guajiro,"
760 said Pulowi to the girls, the daughters of Juya.

Pulowi of the sea was very rich.
Her house was very big, very high.
She had vast quantities of livestock,
she had turtles, fishes, and every kind of sea bird.

765 Si'a stayed in her abode.
A hammock was hung up for him
in which he could lie.

On the third day, at dawn,
when everyone was asleep,
770 he flew up above the jewel bags
hanging very high up, beneath the roof of the house.
He examined them.

One was small,
but it contained the finest jewels.
775 "This is the one I'll take,"
he said to himself.

As soon as he had come back down
he resumed the form of a Guajiro
and stretched out in his hammock.

780 The following night
he was the only one not to go to bed late.
Finally everyone went to sleep.
The old ones slept and snored.
Pulowi was asleep.

785   Si'a observed the *susus,*
    —the woven bags that contained the jewels.
    "Where is this one tied?
    Is it tied up with that one?"
    he wondered.
790   He went and detached the little bag,
    the bag that was fixed in two places to the roof.
    He put it on his shoulder
    and he fled.

    He took it off to Pulowi of the land
795   who was also Juya's wife.

    When Pulowi of the sea awoke
    she looked in the direction of her jewel bags.
    She saw that her bags were no longer there.
    They were scattered on the ground.
800   The smallest one, the most precious one, had vanished.

    Pulowi could no longer see the Guajiro.
    She went and touched his hammock.
    It was empty.
    "Oh! Help me!" she exclaimed.
805   "That man has left with my little woven bag!"

    The daughters of Pulowi awoke.
    "Weren't you with him?"
    they asked her.
    "Yes I was, but he seemed to be asleep.
810   I didn't notice a thing . . ."
    "What are we going to do?" said Pulowi.
    "The bag is already far away,"
    the girls replied.

    Pulowi set the sea in pursuit of the Guajiro.
815   "*Ou! Ouuuuuuu! Ou! Ouuuuuuuuu . . . !*"
    (She always does that when she is robbed.)
    The sea frothed and ran behind him
    but he was already far away.
    The sea could no longer reach him.

820   Si'a was already drawing near to Pulowi of the land.

    "So, have you brought me them?"
    she asked as soon as he arrived.
    "Take this bag!
    In it you'll find her finest gems,"
825   replied the *si'a* bird.

"Let me look," said Pulowi.

From the jewel bag she took out *tu'umas*,
and many necklaces, *kakuunas* and *korolos*.
She dropped them one by one into her net.

830   To the *si'a* bird
Pulowi handed back the bag used to carry them.
"Take it!
Of this bag from the far-off lands, make your hammock,"
she said to him.

835   Since that time
the *si'a* bird possesses a very fine woven straw hammock.

Do you know that bird's nest, *alijuna*?
Have you seen the house of the *si'a* bird?
Hanging up, it looks like a woven bag,
840   a bag that's been stretched at the bottom.
We call it *chirana*.[18]
It was given him by Pulowi.

(Recounted by Shatüi Uliyu, alias José del Carmen, on January 18,
1970, and July 13, 1973. Aged about seventy, he was a stock breeder at
Kasusain, in Venezuelan Guajira. He died in January 1975.)

Do you know, *alijuna*, that Pulowi also eats men?

She devours mainly those who are good deerhunters
845   because she is the mistress of game animals.
She devours them so as to make them her husbands.
This is how it happens:
One day the man does not come back home.
His wife waits for him, one day, two days . . .
850   She sets off in search of him
but she finds no trace, no footprint.
He never comes back,
for he has gone off with Pulowi.
He lives underground with her.
855   Over there, in her domain, there is every kind of food . . .

Pulowi of the sea devours fishermen
and hunters of turtles.
She makes them her husbands.
Every day, every day,
860   they bring back many fishes, or turtles,
two or three that they catch with harpoon or net.

Then, suddenly, they catch nothing more.
Nothing,
only sea.
865 The days go by . . .
Nothing.
Hunger arrives . . .
One day they don't come back.
They never come back again.
870 They have been dragged beneath the sea
by a large skate
or an enormous turtle.
They have been eaten by Pulowi
because they were destroying her stock of game.

875 But Pulowi may also devour any man,
including those who neither hunt nor fish.
She may even lure women
and make them vanish.

Some people have returned from Pulowi's abode,
880 but not for long.
She has always devoured them once more,
and they have never come back again.

This is the story of a shepherd who disappeared:

THE PULOWI OF MATUJAI

Nayalaala Matujainkasa Püloui erein,
885 *nantakaka süma'anam in . . .*
A man had gone near to Matujai.
He had gone to look for his cattle,
to bring them back.
But a Pulowi lived there,
890 a wife of Juya.

The man met her.
She had a girl's appearance,
she smelled good like all the Pulowis.
She lured him into her stone house . . .

895 There she opened her legs.
She wanted to lie with him.

At first he was unwilling,
then he mounted her.

He made her his wife.
900   Juya's wives are all like that . . .

The man stayed there for many days,
one moon and more,
coupling with her.
He had all he wanted.
905   He was given all kinds of food.

"How many people live with you?"
Pulowi asked him one day.
"I have many kinfolk, many nephews,"
the man answered.
910   "Take them all this," she said.
She gave him an enormous pile of *tu'umas*,
marine stones
which women say are the jewels of Juya.
All she'd had to do was pick them up.

915   Then Pulowi let him go.

But when he got home,
the man no longer had anything to say to his wife
nor to his family.
He gave them the jewels.
920   "Now I am off,
I came merely to bring you this."

"Where are you going?" they asked him.
"I live far away
in a land you do not know."

925   The man set off again.

For the second time,
Pulowi devoured him.
He never came back again.

(Story told by Ramansita Uliyu on July 18, 1973. This man, who is
about sixty years old, is a stock breeder at Makalaitpao, in
Colombian Guajira.)

I know a Guajiro who had the same adventure.
930   He did not die straight away,
for he refused to couple with Pulowi.
He stayed with her a long time
but he did not possess her.
He refused all she gave him to eat.

935   One day she let him leave.
      All who act like him can come back.

      Now listen to this story, *alijuna*, foreigner,
      the story of a man devoured by the Pulowi of Ouysimalu.
      An old shaman told it to me.

PULOWI AND THE DEERHUNTER

940   *Eshi wane wayu kusina, olojui irama washiru*
      kepiashi Ouitpanajachi . . .
      There was a *kusina* Indian,
      a great hunter of deer.
      He lived near Ouitpana mountain.
945   He had three children.

      He hunted the deer,
      but also the brocket, the fox, the anteater, the iguana . . .
      He brought back honey.
      In his home he ate wild fruit.
950   His wife removed the skins,
      then she scraped them and put them out to dry.
      She used deer and other animals
      for stews and dried meat.

      These Guajiros did not know hunger.
955   Their loincloths were made of deer hide.
      His was of woven strips,
      his wife's of very soft stitched skin.

      The man went off to hunt very early in the morning.
      Sometimes he brought back two deer, sometimes three.
960   Every day, every day.
      He killed countless deer.
      He was very fond of hunting.

      But one day he no longer sighted anything.
      The deer had gone into hiding,
965   the brocket had gone into hiding,
      the anteaters, the rabbits had gone into hiding,
      the iguanas, the lizards had gone into hiding . . .

      He came back when Jolotsü, the planet Venus, appeared,
      with hunger, with thirst.

970   All the animals had vanished.
      Pulowi kept them with her.

This lasted for many days.
His children cried from hunger.
His wife cooked the fat that was left.
975   She boiled the deer hides.
Then she chewed them
and gave them to the children to eat.

The man went off into the bush with his axe,
in search of honey.
980   But there was no longer any honey.
He no longer saw anything, anything at all.
Everything had vanished.

This lasted a long time, a very long time.
"What can I do now?" said the man.

985   He looked for torch cacti laden with figs.
He would spend the night there.
If deer came up to eat the fruit
he would pierce them with his arrows.

"I'll go and sleep there.
990   I shall not return until I have killed something.
Count the days of my absence.
If I hunt nothing
I shall never come back.
I don't wish to see my children suffering any more,"
995   said the man to his wife before leaving.

He went to Oulekimana, near to Ouysimalu,
on the way to a *pulowi* land.
The moon was high.
The night was calm.

1000   Once there, he hid among the cacti
armed with his arrows.
Soon a large white deer came toward him.
It had huge antlers
in which two *seruma* birds were nesting.

1005   "Here it comes!
Whatever it is, I'll pierce it with my arrow.
Even if it changes into a snake on the ground,
even if it is *wanülü*,
I shall eat it.
1010   Even if I find in its place a girl stretched out,
I shall eat it.
Because for me, it is a deer!"

The deer started eating the fruit of the cacti.
The man prepared his bow.
1015　He shot an arrow at it.
The deer leapt into the air and ran off,
falling down a short distance away,
the arrow firmly planted in a shoulder.

The man shot another arrow.
1020　He hit a leg.
The deer went down.
The man rushed toward it.
But before he had time to reach it,
the deer raced off again,
1025　with the two arrows in it,
falling down a short distance away,
its neck bent over under its body.
"This time it's going to die!"
The man seized hold of a stick to beat it to death.
1030　But once again
the deer rose to its feet before the man could reach it.
It started running once more, swerving from side to side.
The man, chasing after it again,
followed close behind.

1035　Suddenly
the deer passed beneath a stone.
The man rushed after it.
The deer sank into the earth.
The man fell in after it . . .

1040　Now the deer was reclining beneath a sunroof.
It had assumed human form.

The man stood nearby.
From all sides girls and women emerged.
There were vast numbers of them.
1045　Some had very short hair,
some had longer hair,
some had huge manes
that reached all the way down to their knees.
All wore countless necklaces.

1050　"Is he my brother or my maternal uncle?
Is he my father or my paternal uncle?
He'll tell me when he recounts his story to me.
When the shadows are longer
I shall come and talk with him.

1055   For the time being, bring him a hammock,"
        said Pulowi to those around her.

        Around her many women were gathered.
        They brought a sisal hammock
        for the Guajiro who had just arrived.
1060   Two of them hung it up.
        "Lie down!"
        They unfolded the hammock.
        The man stretched out.
        He kept his metal arrows.
1065   He placed his bow across his knees.

        He was very hungry.
        Beans were brought to him, in a large dish.
        He refused to eat them.
        He was offered watermelon.
1070   He didn't want to taste it.
        He was given new corn.
        He refused it.
        They tried to tempt him with ground corn and cheese.
        Nothing doing!

1075   "What do you want to eat?
        You are with us now, cease your suffering.
        Since you have no wife here,
        you'll be our husband,"
        the young women said to the Guajiro.
1080   "I didn't come looking for women!
        I came to see if I could be saved.
        That's what I want," he replied.

        The girls the man saw were brockets.
        Those he took for women were deer,
        rabbits, and foxes . . .

1085   "Where are the corrals of these rich women?"
        The man looked around him.
        He saw paddocks, a succession of paddocks,
        some full of sheep,
        others of goats,
1090   others of cows,
        others reserved for mules and horses.
        Saddles there were in great numbers.

        Late in the evening Pulowi came out.
        The Guajiro saw a rich woman arrive,

1095 a very rich woman, immensely rich.
She wore jewels on her ankles,
gold chains around her wrists.

"Here comes Pulowi! It is she!
What will happen to me?
1100 Who cares! I'll do anything.
I don't want to see my children suffer."

"Yes, I am Pulowi. What do you want from me?"
Without hearing him,
she knew what the Guajiro had said.
1105 "I'll call you younger brother.
You would seem very old and ugly
if I called you brother of my mother,"[19]
she added.
They spoke for a long time together.

1110 Two days passed in this way.
The Guajiro's wife wept.
Perhaps something has happened to him.
Perhaps he has hanged himself,
she thought.

1115 She set out in search of him,
following his footprints.
But they could be seen only around the house.
Further on, in the bush, they had vanished.

There the man no longer knew what to do.
1120 He was very hungry.
But if he had eaten some watermelon,
he would have become a rabbit.
If he had eaten beans or corn,
he would have become a deer.
1125 He would have been the does' husband.

On account of his hunger,
his *heart* had lost all its strength.

He had brought some tobacco with him,
yüi makuira tobacco,
1130 the tobacco used by shamans.
It was in a box,
stowed away in the woven bag he carried on his arm.
The man took it out.
He broke off a small piece
1135 and put it in his mouth.

He chewed it.
He swallowed the juice.
He felt one of his arms going to sleep.
"This is what happens to shamans," he said to himself.

1140   He chewed a second piece.
He kept the juice in his mouth.
"*Sulum! Sulum! Sulum!* . . ."
He spat it into the air.

At once the deer started running,
1145   this way, that way, in every direction.
Those who previously were women
suddenly became rabbits, deer . . .
simply from smelling the tobacco *yüi makuira*.

"What is it that smells so bad?" asked Pulowi.
1150   The stench had drifted all the way over to her.
"It's your younger brother who smells so foul,"
said a brocket.

Pulowi sent for the Guajiro.
She was frightened of him,
1155   for the smell of the tobacco *yüi* is forbidden to Pulowis:
pülasü ma'i shejü yüi sümüin Püloui.
It is very dangerous for them.
It has supernatural powers against them.

"What have you got in your mouth, younger brother?"
1160   said Pulowi from the sunroof.
She was frightened,
she would not approach him.

"So that you stop hurting me
I'm going to arrange for you to return home,
1165   but in fine fashion.
I shall give you a robe and a handsome belt,
I shall give you shoes,
I shall give you a horse,
I shall give you fine jewels.
1170   This is what I shall do for you.
I know that you have three children,
a girl, a young man, and a small boy.
I know your wife.
I shall arrange for you to be taken to them.
1175   And yet, because of you, I have lost many livestock.
Young women have been lost.

Young men, old folk, have been lost.
He who brought you here is one of my maternal uncles.
He is over there.
1180 The arrows you shot at him will not come out.
Go and pull them out of him."

But already the smell of the tobacco was upsetting Pulowi.
"Leave at once, at once I say!" she exclaimed.
"But be careful,
1185 do not go and say:
I am back from Pulowi's abode.
Do not recount what you have seen here.
If you wish to stay as you are,
keep the secret for a period of one year.
1190 If you say what has happened to you,
I shall not help you.
Otherwise, when you are in need,
I shall send you animals that you'll be able to eat."

Pulowi let the Guajiro leave.

1195 He emerged beside the torch cacti,
those by which he had disappeared.
At their foot two deer were coupling.
He pierced them with his arrows and carried them both off.

Already the man's *heart* was beating more strongly.

2000 Laden with game,
he arrived home.
It was already late.
When she saw him coming,
his wife began to weep.

2005 "Do not weep at my return.
I merely fell asleep,
for I met with nothing.
Do not weep but prepare the fire."

The woman made the fire.
2010 The man cut up the deer.
His children were sleeping on the ground, without hammocks,
sad and hungry.

The next day, before dawn,
the man went off hunting.
2015 He brought back a deer.
At noon he set off again.

He came back with a brocket.

He did this every day.
He went and sat down, over there,
2020   next to the place where the Pulowi lived.
He did not see her,
but for him the animals fell silent,
the animals that are found in *pulowi* lands.

Every day the man came back laden with game.
2025   But he was the only one to find any.
His kin no longer killed anything.
He fed all his family.
To some he gave a shoulder,
to others a leg,
2030   but they never met with anything.
He alone found honey, rabbits, foxes,
and all the animals the Guajiro eat.

One day, however, much later,
the man disappeared again,
2035   with his wife and children.
He had gone back under the earth
like the first time.

It is said that he sometimes comes out
in the form of a completely white deer.
2040   He is called Katoule, "he who has much skin."
By his broad tracks
he can be recognized.

He can take on human appearance.
He transpierces dogs.
2045   He threatens men.

He has become a *wanülü*.

Over there, around the Pulowi of Ouysimalu,
cows can now be seen.
They are in stone,
2050   but they are Pulowi's animals.
Recumbent bulls can be seen
with their horns, which are in stone.
They are squeezed up against one another, countless.
In the ground, hard as stone,
2055   there are horses' saddles, irons for branding cattle,
now all made of stone.
For Pulowi is very rich.

Her house is like a rich *alijuna's* dwelling.
It is made of several contiguous buildings,
2060 all in stone.
Like all houses, it has a door.
It is a hole between the stones.
Pulowi lives below.

Over there, in that place, many *julua* trees grow,
2065 and countless iguanas live,
hummingbirds in large numbers,
and all kinds of wild animals.

(Recounted by Setuma Pushaina, alias José Tomás Palmar, on August
11, 1973. This man, who was about fifty years old, was a shaman. He
lived at Jawo, east of Uribia, in Colombian Guajira. He died in July
1975, murdered.)

Do you know what a *wanülü* is, foreigner?

Some say that Wanülü is Pulowi's brother,
2070 others claim that he is her maternal uncle.
However it may be, they are kin.
Wanülü, sülaüla Püloui, papüshawasü . . .

The *wanülüs* are invisible, and they do not speak.
Those who see them are those who are about to die.
2075 When they advance face on, riding their mules,
the *wanülüs* resemble *alijunas*.
They wear black or white garments,
like *alijunas*.
Often their hats shine,
2080 as do their guns and their rings.

Careful! say the Guajiro,
A *wanülü* has just stopped,
he is standing there.
Look to your children!
2085 Tell them to be quiet!
Do you not hear him whistling?
Whish! Whish! Ui! Ui! . . .
Prepare your arrows! . . .

The *wanülüs* who kill the Guajiro appear mainly at night.
2090 They come out when the sun is very low.
Darkness is theirs.
We meet them when we walk at night.

Those who get up before dawn die because of them,
as do those who walk around at nightfall.

2095   When a *wanülü* has pierced you with his arrow,
there is no remedy.
A *wanülü* is like the hunter who kills the deer:
he shoots his arrow at us, whistling *vi! vi!* . . .
Then he goes off in search of another victim.
3000   It is said that he sees us in the form of deer.

The *wanülüs* belong to the land
and the land is theirs:
wanülüjai, nükorolo tü makat.
Often a *wanülü* assumes the appearance of an *animal.*[20]
3005   When a Guajiro manages to kill him,
with his bow and arrows,
he finds him in the form of a snake.
But sometimes he can also turn into a fox,
a rabbit, a dog,
3010   or even a bird,
especially an urubu.

Listen to this story, *alijuna.*
My grandfather told it to me.
He knew very well the hunter who was its hero.

THE DEERHUNTER, THE *WANÜLÜ*, AND THE SHAMAN

3015   *Eshi wane olojui irama . . .*
This is the story of a deerhunter.
His wife and daughter always went with him.
They shouted to make the deer come out.
The hunter waited further on, with his arrows,
3020   near the place where they had left their tracks.
(The deer always followed the same path;
their footprints could be seen on the ground.
There he lay in wait for them.)

One day,
3025   when the women were shouting to drive out the deer,
the *wanülü* was standing there,
waiting for them.

He was dressed in black, completely in black.
He resembled a hunter,
3030   but he was a *wanülü.*

"*Kama! Kama! Kama!*"
the girl shouted to bring out the deer.
She was the first to come out of the coppice.
The *wanülü* was there, on the lookout.
3035 He shot an arrow at her.

At the same moment,
her father, the hunter, saw a doe fall.
It was his daughter who had assumed for him the appearance
    of a doe.
The *wanülü* had killed her.

3040 The woman came next.
The *wanülü* killed her
in front of her husband, who was waiting for the deer.

Immediately afterward
the girl came in sight of her father.
3045 She stumbled and fell
there where the doe had been killed.
Then she set off again.
The mother came next.
She stumbled and fell in the same place.

3050 All three of them set off back to the house.
They walked.
The woman carried fruit from the *yosu* cactus.

But, when they arrived,
the hunter did not want to eat.
3055 He was frightened.
He was not sure that the man he had seen was a *wanülü*.
He could have been a hunter like himself.
But now he had doubts.
When he had noticed that man,
3060 he had felt a *force* in his body,
he had had to lower his head.
The man had immediately hidden himself
and he had not seen him any more.
It was then that his wife and daughter had come along.
3065 And perhaps already it was no longer they
but only their flesh and skin
that had come all the way to the house.

First the daughter started to bleed.
She brought up a lot of blood,
3070 then she dropped dead.

Immediately afterward the mother spat blood,
then she died.
The *wanülü* had killed the two women.

The hunter buried them beneath his house,
3075 as people used to do in earlier times.
then he went and saw a diviner,
a very learned Guajiro,
who was also a shaman.

"I have come to see you, grandfather,
3080 to ask you to divine what is happening to me.
My wife is dead, my daughter is dead,
and I am going mad."

The hunter gave him a gold pendant,
gave him brandy and a mule
3085 as fee for his divining.

"This is something very bad!
We are dealing with a fierce *wanülü*.
You saw yourself what happened:
the *wanülü* killed them in front of you.
3090 You saw them fall.
You could have shot an arrow at him straight away.
Now he would be dead."
"I thought he was a person,"
said the hunter.

3095 When the shaman had finished divining
they set off for the hunter's place,
there where the two dead women were buried.
There the old man started divining again.

At nightfall they went off.
4000 They walked for a long time.
The following morning
they arrived near the place where the *wanülü* was.
It was almost noon.
"He lives here! We are very close to his abode!"
4005 said the shaman, who was also a diviner.

The *wanülü* was in a tree trunk.
It was a very thick one
but at the top there was a hole.
The *wanülü* was there.

4010 "Stay there!"

said the shaman to the dead woman's husband.
He went toward the tree.
He had a machete.
He hit the trunk with it.

4015   "He's there! He is sleeping! He is snoring!"
It was noon.
"Tun! Tun! Tun! Tun!"
The *wanülü* was snoring very loudly.
The shaman went back to hitting the trunk.

4020   "Be careful! Kill everything that comes out!"
"Tun! Tun! Tun!"
The *wanülü* slept.

Suddenly an urubu flew off.
The hunter shot an arrow at it and killed it.
4025   *Pshwitt!* It fell down further on.
The two men ran off.

"I shall start divining again,"
said the shaman when they had gone far enough away.
"There's still his wife," he said.
4030   "She is ferocious.
She is coming toward us.
Kill her, no matter what form she has taken!"

The *wanülü's* wife drew near.
She came out
4035   in the form of a vixen who has recently given birth.
Her udders hung down.
The hunter killed her at once.
"And the little foxes?" he asked.
"Leave them in their hole.
4040   It's not worth the trouble burning them,
they'll die of hunger,"
the diviner replied.

"What does it look like, what we have killed?"
they wondered later.
4045   In the place of the vixen
they found a large white snake with black spots,
called *kasiwanou.*
"Let's go to the place where we killed her husband."
There they found a *sarulu*, a boa.

4050   Later,

there where the mother and her daughter had been buried,
iguanas and snakes of all kinds emerged,
offspring of the two women taken by the *wanülü*,
süchon wayu, saapain wanülü.
4055   Every day,
they emerged from their graves.

(Recounted by Salachon Aapshana, alias Luis González, on February 1, 1970. Salachon is a fisherman aged about fifty living at Pararu, in Venezuelan Guajira.)

I told you so, *alijuna*, foreigner,
the *wanülüs* are very fierce,
and when you meet them
4060   it is very rare to be able to get away.
But I know a shepherd who was faster than a *wanülü* . . .

A SHEPHERD KILLS A *WANÜLÜ*

Nüchükua wane wayu ekajirüi annerü, wayu jimai . . .
There was a Guajiro,
a young man who took his sheep out to graze.
4065   Every day, around noon,
he rested in the shade of a cassia tree with his flock,
near a dried-up river bed.

One day, when he reached the cassia tree, around noon,
he noticed that a lamb had vanished.
4070   "I'll go and look for it at once,
or else the foxes will eat it."
The young man retraced his steps.
He followed the tracks of his flock.

Soon he saw somebody walking along by the tracks
4075   in the same direction as himself.
It was a man carrying a rifle on his shoulder.
He was like a hunter.
The shepherd stopped to look at him.
Like him, the man was following the tracks of the flock.
4080   Soon he disappeared in the distance, in the river bed.
The shepherd started walking again along by the tracks.
He found the lamb.
He caught it and held its mouth closed
so that it would not bleat.

4085 He came straight back to where he had hung his hammock,
     near the river bed, beneath the cassia tree.
     The sun was very hot.
     The young man was tired.
     He fell asleep.

4090 Suddenly, he was awakened by a dream.
     "Do not sleep! A man is after you!
     A *wanülü* is coming!
     He whom you saw earlier is a *wanülü!*
     If you want to see him,
4095 take the rheum from your dog's eyes
     and eat it!
     Thus you will be able to see the *wanülü,*
     as the dog can see him,"
     a woman said to him, in a dream,
5000 and she shook his hammock.

     At once the young man leaned out of the hammock.
     His little dog was lying next to him.
     From the corner of its eyes he took some rheum
     and he swallowed it.
5005 He sprang at once to his feet.
     From behind him the *wanülü* was approaching.
     He resembled an *alijuna.*
     He was carrying a rifle.

     The Guajiro hid.
5010 He had but a bow and arrows,
     two *siwarai* arrows, with metal tips,
     mounted on olive wood.
     The *wanülü* aimed at the hammock.
     Very fast the Guajiro shot an arrow at him.
5015 The *wanülü* flew off,
     as though he were a bird, a black heron.
     He dropped dead some distance off, in the coppice.

     The following night the young man dreamed.
     "You are safe!
5020 The man who was following your tracks is dead.
     Now, at nighttime,
     look toward where the dogs are barking.
     You will see all that they see,"
     the dream said to him . . .

(Recounted by Kashükemasü Jayaliyu, alias Francisco Fernandez, on September 6, 1969. This man, who is about sixty years old, is a stock breeder at Pararu, in Venezuelan Guajira.)

5025   Sometimes, *alijuna*, foreigner,
it even happens that a shaman, a very powerful shaman,
is able to cure a sick person pierced by a *wanülü*'s arrow.
Listen to this story, recounted by the elders:

A GIRL PIERCED BY A *WANÜLÜ*'S ARROW IS CURED BY A SHAMAN

Nantaka wanülü sünain wayu majayülü . . .
5030   A *wanülü* came near a Guajiro girl
one evening, at dusk.
She was walking
as though she had wanted to meet him
and he pierced her with his arrow.

5035   The next morning
she was very sick.
She stayed in bed all day
but she did not die.
The *wanülü* had not yet eaten her.
5040   He had merely wounded her.

Nearby there lived a woman who was a shaman.
She was brought to where the sick girl lay.
It was nighttime.

The shaman began to chant
5045   and to shake her rattle.
"Pshuuu! . . . Pshuuu! . . ."
she sang, spitting out chewed tobacco juice.
"I have seen him, it's a *wanülü!*"
she said, leaving the sick girl.
5050   *"Taye! . . . Teyaye! . . ."*
The girl wailed.
She was in great pain.

The following night
the shaman began to chant again.
5055   "The *wanülü* isn't here, beside her.
When he pierced her the first time,
death did not come.

He wasn't able to take away her *soul*,
but now he is getting ready to eat her.
5060   He will do so tonight
or another night.
He will come for her in her house,"
said the shaman to the sick girl's parents.

"Night draws near.
5065   You must prepare to encounter him,"
she said to the girl, to the *wanülü*'s victim.
She was shut up in a little house.

The shaman began chanting again
and shaking the rattle.
5070   "Over there is a heap of clay.
From there will emerge an *alijuna*, a foreigner.
He will come looking for the girl.
She will recognize him when he stands up,"
her *spirits* said to her.

5075   "He wants to kill you!
Go over there, behind this large piece of cloth,"
said the shaman to the sick girl,
who was lying in a hammock,
hidden between two pieces of cloth attached to the roof.
5080   The shaman was on the other side.
In the opposite corner she had a man concealed,
armed with a bow and arrows.

Early in the night,
the *wanülü* arrived,
5085   like an *alijuna*.
He had come in search of the one he had wounded.
He wanted to carve her up.

The house was small and entirely closed.
The *wanülü* rose up along the wall.
5090   The hunter was waiting for him.
He was in a good position.
Schok! went the *siwarai*, the metal arrow.

There was a spark
like when a fire is lit.
5095   For the *wanülü* the house was not hard
and he passed through it, near the main beam.
Blood fell on the Guajiro who was beneath.
The *alijuna* had been well and truly transpierced,

under the arms.
6000 For the arrow was very long.
It came crashing down far away.
Sparks came out of it.
This was how his blood appeared.
The hunter's body was painted with blood.

6005 They did not go to collect the arrow:
it was night,
they were frightened.

The next morning they saw no trace.
The house was not damaged,
6010 it was as before.

The arrow had fallen among *julua* trees.
They went to get it.
They found a huge *kasiwanou* snake,
stretched out lifeless,
6015 with the barbed arrow planted in its middle.

"What shall we do with it?"
"Better leave it," they said.
No one wanted to pull out the arrow,
and so they left it.

6020 The girl was alive.
She felt better since the *wanülü* had died.
If they had not stuck an arrow in the *wanülü*,
she would not be alive anymore.

But the *wanülüs* can die too . . .

(Recounted by Salachon Aapshana on September 8, 1969.)

6025 Do you know Jamü—Hunger—*alijuna?*
Like Wanülü
—some say he is his son or his brother—
Hunger pierces the Guajiro with his arrows.
Like a *wanülü*, he assumes the appearance of a snake.

6030 Hunger attacks the livestock first,
when the dry season comes, the *jamü-jouktai:*
the time of wind and hunger.
It can last eight moons,
nine moons, sometimes ten moons.
6035 Then all the animals die of thirst

and men too are threatened by hunger and sickness.

Listen to this story, *alijuna:*

HUNGER ATTACKS

Antatüta jouktai joo'o
aiiisü jamü, atkajüi jamü.
6040 *O'onosü wayu chaya wopumüin . . .*
Jouktai—the east wind—has arrived.
Ay! Hunger grows, Hunger invades all,
Hunger attacks!
The Guajiro seek pasture land.
6045 They make their way yonder, westward.

An Indian stops on the way.
Two of his animals have disappeared.
They have fallen behind,
they have lain down to die.

6050 They have to be skinned, for their hides.

But already, further on,
another cow collapses,
then another, here . . .

Someone comes behind the Guajiro
6055 by the same path.
A man he has already encountered.
Naked, he holds a bow in his hand.
He follows the footprints of the animals,
he shoots his arrows at them.
6060 It is he who makes them lie down,
and die.
When he draws near he starts shouting,
as the Guajiro do to hail one another from afar.
"He must be a man, then,"
6065 the Indian says to himself.

The man has few arrows.
But as he shoots them at the footprints
he can take them back each time.

When he is closer to the Guajiro,
6070 he shouts again,
a huge shout.
The Guajiro hides.

The man follows the path.
He stops, leans over,
6075   shoots arrows at other footprints,
each time once.

Suddenly he vanishes:
someone else comes along the path.

The Guajiro comes out of his hiding place.
6080   But again he hears the shout,
a shout that comes from far, far away.

"Why shoot arrows at footprints?
Why shoot arrows into the earth?"
he wonders.
6085   He goes toward the spot where the man stopped.
Nothing can be seen,
only the footprints of cows.

In his body the Guajiro has felt the force,
as when one meets a *wanülü*,
6090   but he does not know why.

In the evening he returns to his shelter.[21]
"Kayamülasü tata nütuma:
I have felt the force in my body!
I must return with my herd,"
6095   he says to the relatives who live with him.

He arrives at dawn.
He finishes skinning his dead cows.
When day breaks
he goes off to rejoin his herd.

7000   His finest bull is dead.
His cows totter,
then drop dead.
But soon
he must stop opening bodies
7005   and recovering the hides:

He is coming back.
Hunger is already coming back.

(Recounted by Salachon Aapshana on November 16, 1969.)

You know, *alijuna,*
joukataleulu—the dry season—
7010   can be terrible for the Guajiro.

One or two moons after the rains of Iiwa
—the constellation of the Pleiades—
the Guajiro start digging wells
within the large dried-up pools.
7015   In this way they find water, drunk by men and animals.

But when the rains of Iiwa have been bad,
they have to start digging a long time before.
And at the approach of the rains of Juyo'u
—the star Arcturus—
7020   the wells are very deep and difficult of access.

When the grass has gone,
when the herds no longer find anything to eat,
the men have to leave with their cattle,
in search of better lands:
7025   *o'onooshi wayu.*

When there is no water left in the wells,
the Guajiro families go away too,
to avoid death.
Sometimes they go away and do not come back:
7030   *okojoloshi wayu.*
Somewhere else they have found better land,
a land where the grass stays green for longer,
a land where hunger is less cruel.[22]

Drought is the enemy of the Guajiro.
7035   It is drought that brings hunger.
Anxiously the Guajiro wait for *juyapu,*
the rainy season, the period of Juya.
"Here is the thunder of Iruala,
the thunder of the star Spica,
7040   time for us to sow!
Soon we shall have a crop of beans,
millet, watermelons, and muskmelons.
Here is the thunder of Juyo'u,
we'll be able to eat our fill,"
7045   say the Guajiro when the rains come.

Do you know what we do, *alijuna,*
in some regions of Guajira,
to make the rain fall?

THE HOLES OF THE *YALAMÜNA* IGUANAS

At Wüinpümüin, in Upper Guajira,
7050   near Talwayupana, there is a *pulowi* place.
At night, lightning can be seen.
In the daytime, one can find *yalamünas*,
a kind of iguana with a forked tail
that continually swings its head from side to side.
7055   Under their necks they have a pouch, and they take fright
             very easily.
As soon as you approach them, they go back into the earth.
It is difficult to catch them.[23]

It is said that they stop the rain from falling.
7060   Juya will not come if their holes are not blocked up,
those holes through which the *yalamüna* iguanas come out.

During the dry season, when food becomes scarce,
people gather together.
Before filling in the holes,
7065   they prepare a feast.
Some bring sheep, others coffee, others tobacco.
The men use sand,
earth, and even rubbish,
to fill the holes of the *yalamüna* iguanas.
7070   Corn beer is drunk.
The *yonna* is danced.

When all the holes have been blocked,
the *yalamüna* iguanas can no longer come out,
and the rain makes an appearance.
7075   If it's not the next day,
it will be in a few days,
or in a moon.
But if the holes were not blocked
it would not rain at all.

(Recounted by Makantre Uliana on February 8, 1970. A fisherman,
aged about fifty, he lived at Kousharaichon, in Venezuelan Guajira.)

THE RAIN AND THE HOLES OF THE *JOKOCHES*

7080   Near Neimalu, too, there is a *pulowi* land.
At night, this *pulowi* sends lightning.
In the daytime she is inhabited by *jokoches*

—brown lizards that fling their heads forward
and swell out the large red and yellow pouch on their necks,
7085   in the direction of the lightning, before it rains.
One year, it had not rained over there for a very long time.
My maternal uncle, an old man,
woke up hungrier every day.
All he took was water,
7090   for there was nothing to eat.

One day a man came to see him and said:
"Why do you sleep?
You see those holes over here,
they are preventing the rain of Juyo'u from falling.
7095   They have to be blocked up.
Let's get some men together.
Let's fill in the holes of the *jokoches*.
That's where Pulowi comes out.

Some Indians began throwing stones,
8000   sand, and rubble into the *pulowi*.
Others collected food:
all that was left in the way of millet, beans,
watermelon seeds, gourd seeds . . .
Someone even gave a small bull.
8005   It was killed immediately.
A *yonna* dance was organized, people began to dance.

When all the holes were filled,
clouds arrived.
It rained from noon to dawn.

8010   Immediately seeds were collected
and everybody went off to sow.

Because they did that,
these people did not die.

(Recounted by Matewa Jitnu on October 6, 1969. This stock breeder,
who is close to eighty years old, lives at Kousharaichon, in
Venezuelan Guajira.)

Nünü'ükat Juya tü Pülouikat . . .
8015   Pulowi is the enemy of Juya,
and it is she who stops the rain from falling.

When the thunder starts rumbling,
when the land where we are starts to shake,
this means that Juya is drawing near her abode.

8020   But this is also said:
Rainbow is the one who stands in the way of the rain . . .

RAINBOW

Nojolüin kasipoluinka wanepiaerüsü tü juyaka eitüin . . .
Without Kasipoluin, the Rainbow, it would rain continually.
But Rainbow has come to tell Juya to stop.
8025   She has come to scatter the rains.

Rainbow comes out at the same time as Juya,
to advise him to hold himself back:
"Stop raining, Juya," she says to him.

Rainbow is said to be the tongue of a snake,
8030   a snake living inside the earth, like a root.
What comes out of its mouth, like smoke, is threefold:
wüitüsü, malaukatsü, ishosü
—green or blue, yellow and red.
But the snake itself is single.
8035   Its colors are the colors of its emanations.

I know a child who, while running,
went to the place where a rainbow emerged.
He saw a snake curled up.
Frightened, he took to his heels.
8040   He did not try to go near it again.
But he really had seen the rainbow come out of a snake.

Furthermore, say the Guajiro,
snakes are the enemies of Juya,
and Juya is the enemy of snakes.
8045   He strikes them with his lightning when he sees them.
It is because of him that all the biggest ones are dead.

(Story by Shatüi Uliyu, recounted on January 29, 1970, at Pararu.)

Some claim that Rainbow always comes out of the *sarulu* boa.
Others say that it can be any other snake,
an iguana, or even the *maliwa* crocodile.

8050   This is what I have been told, *alijuna:*

THE RAINBOW AND THE CROCODILE

A violent storm had broken.
A hunter had taken shelter from the rain,
behind a stone.
Very close to him, he saw the rainbow emerge.
8055 He went toward it on all fours.
He soon saw a *maliwa* crocodile:
from its wide-open mouth the rainbow emerged.
As soon as it was all the way out,
the rain stopped.
8060 The hunter did not dare get any closer,
for he had never seen that before.
He took to his heels.

(Recounted by Mateo Jitnu, on October 6, 1969, at Kousharaichon.)

Every year, however,
when Juyo'u, the star Arcturus,
8065 goes down behind the sun,
the rains sweep across Guajira,
in too great an abundance . . .
Do you know why, *alijuna?*

JUYA'S DEBT

Joutkaka juya kainalajashi Juya,
8070 *asikasü nierüin nüma Iiwa,*
nuutainchi nainchi . . .
The rains are abundant because Juya got into trouble:
his wife coupled with Iiwa,
and so he killed her brother.

8075 Now, to pay for this death,[24]
Juya has to gather people and animals:
nunuakaka Juya, nükochakaka, nüwalajüinjachi.
Because of that there are many sicknesses.
Because of that men and animals die.
8080 To pay for the rains and the pasture lands
the Guajiro and their animals must die:
men give their dead;
in exchange, Juya gives rain to the families of the dead.

Before, hunger was perhaps more rife,

8085   but there was no need to pay back that debt,
that debt which is now paid with the dead.

(Recounted by Mainsain Uliyu, alias Manuel Salvador Fernández, on
January 29, 1970. Aged about forty, this stock breeder lived near
Kasusain, in Venezuelan Guajira. He died in September 1975.)

You see, *alijuna,*
because of Juya's act
there are many diseases in Guajira,
8090   during the rainy season.

All the diseases caused by water
—*ayule sünainjejet wüin*—:
oushua, fever, *shülera,* worms in the feet,
shünüi, fever and coughing, *polona, kochi, . . .*
8095   all these diseases are Juya's companions.

Juya is nothing other than the long-dead Guajiro.
That's why there are so many rains on earth.
Moreover, when it is going to rain,
one dreams of the dead.
9000   The elders have learned this from experience.

However, like Moon, Juya is our father:
müsü kashi, washikai Juya.
Without Juya we would not be here.
He comes with watermelons,
9005   he comes with muskmelons,
he comes with corn . . .
Through him the cows have milk,
through him the pigs grow fat . . .
Moon is our father, say the Guajiro,
9010   *washi kashi, münüshi.*
Without Moon girls would not have their periods,[25]
and without periods, a woman cannot have children.
From that blood the child is fed.

Moon has many women,
9015   Moon takes every woman.

Like Moon,
Juya is very virile.
He has countless children,
all over the earth.
9020   And many are the girls abducted by Juya.
Listen to this story:

A SECLUDED GIRL ABDUCTED BY JUYA

Esü wane wayu majayülü paüsü, pülainrü . . .
This is the story of a secluded girl who was *pülainrü*.
Since her childhood, she had liked to stay cooped up.

9025 One day when it was drizzling
her father and mother went off to sow their garden.
The maidservant remained alone with the girl.

Suddenly huge clouds gathered,
huge clouds in the midst of which a man appeared.
9030 Riding a strong mule
he advanced with the storm.

The maidservant saw him.
He was dressed in black.
His mule was black.

9035 He came right up to the sunroof.
"A man I do not know has just arrived,"
said the maidservant to the girl.
"Hang up a hammock beneath the sunroof and receive him,"
she replied.
9040 "The rain that fell before you came was very violent,"
said the maidservant to the man.
"Nothing strange in that.
Virile men always arrive with the rain.
Since I am a man
9045 I came with the rain.
Where is my younger sister?"
"She is inside."
"Call her. Tell her to come here
for my smell is unpleasant.
9050 It is hot,
and I reek with the smell of my mule.
Tell her not to be frightened, I am her brother.
I got lost when I was small."

The maidservant was frightened.
9055 It seemed to her that the man was not a Guajiro.
She went back into the house
and she repeated what she had just heard.
"I have no brother who got lost.
When would he have gone missing?
9060 But if he is my brother, tell him to come in.
I don't want to go out," said the girl.

"Where is my father? Where is my mother?"
the man asked the servant when she came back.
"They are sowing."
9065   "What! They are sowing in this worthless rain!"[26]

"I'll go and see if he's really my brother."
The girl suddenly decided to go out.

"*Tashunu*, younger sister, don't be frightened. I am your
    brother.
9070   It's you I was looking for."
"Before I come with you,
you must tell my father and mother,"
said the girl.
"Why? We don't need them.
9075   We must set off straightaway."
"I don't want to leave until they get back.
They wouldn't know where to look for me.
My mother would be very upset . . ."
"No. We'll meet them on the way,
9080   and in any case, we'll soon be back,"
replied the man.

"That man is not a Guajiro,"
the servant said to herself, seeing him in such a hurry.
And she went off to warn the parents.

9085   "Let's go!" the girl suddenly said.
shortly after the maidservant had left.

The man immediately took her up behind him,
and slowly the mule set off.
Rain started to fall, the wind started to blow.
9090   They advanced into it on their mount.
The mule rose into the air toward the clouds.
Soon they were very high.

The servant had got to where the parents were.
"Your long-lost son has returned.
9095   He wants to take his sister away.
Come immediately!"

"It's true that one of our sons went missing.
It must be him.
We thought he was dead,
10,000   we didn't think he could still be alive,"
said the father and mother.

They came back in haste,
but it was difficult to run in the rain and wind.
When they arrived,
10,005   the girl was already very far away.
She was over there, very high up . . .
The man who had come to get her was Juya.

(Recounted by Makaerü Jitnu, alias Mikaela Suárez [photograph 10],
on November 2, 1969. This woman, who is about fifty years old, lives
at Pararu, in Venezuelan Guajira.)

Juya is our Father,
Moon is our Father . . .
10,010   But there are Guajiros who also say:
Juya is Maleiwa's son;
nüchon nia Maleiwa tia Juyakai, sümünaka.

Maleiwa is he who made us.
Maleiwa divided us up and gave us clans.
10,015   He gave us cattle and tools . . .

Maleiwa is the grandfather of all the Guajiro,
Maleiwa, born of a woman devoured by Jaguar.

Listen to this last story, recounted by the elders, *alijuna,*
the very long story of Maleiwa:
10,020   a story that dates back a very, very long time ago,
to a time when all things were mixed together on earth,
sümaiwa pülaiwa makat . . .

MALEIWA

Eeshi chii uchii ajuupajüikai jime,
chii kemenülükai, yalaa palairuko . . .

10,025   "Sea hawk" is the bird who swims very well,
who drops down on fish to catch them.[27]
Before, he was a man.
He enjoyed fishing very much.
Every day he brought back fish.

10,030   His wife gave him a daughter.
The little girl grew up.
Her father was very fond of her.

When she had her first period
she went into seclusion.

10,035 She was locked up in a little house.
When she came out
she was a young woman.[28]

She then discovered that she was pregnant.
No one knew who had made her so.
10,040 When her father realized,
her belly was already very big.
"Who made you this child?" he asked her.
"I do not know.
No man has ever come to see me.
10,045 It took shape by itself in my womb."

When she was very big,
the child began to talk.
"Make me some arrows,
I want to go hunting,"
10,050 he said when she passed before a *koushot* tree.
"What could he do with an arrow,
and how could he go hunting,
since he is still in my womb?"
his mother wondered.

10,055 But the child badgered her.
She cut him an arrow.
But he did not come out.
He went on talking.

Then, weary of hearing and answering him,
10,060 his mother struck herself on the belly.
The child was displeased and stopped talking.
"Come out, since you are a hunter," she shouted at him.
But he remained silent.

One day when she had gone off to cut some wood
10,065 a splinter fell in her eye and burst it.
Immediately the other eye stopped seeing.

The woman was blind.
She could no longer see the world.
She walked haphazardly . . .
10,070 She took the wrong path
and she lost her way in the bush.
She could no longer find her house.
The child was in her womb,
but he did not want to talk.
10,075 She slept outside on the ground.

She walked for a long time, a very long time . . .

Thus she came to where Jaguar's mother lived.[29]
Jaguar was out hunting.
"Ai . . . *tachon nee!* Ooh, my daughter!"
10,080   said Jaguar's mother, taking her by the arm.
She led her to her home.
The woman had walked for two days.
She was very hungry.
Jaguar's mother gave her something to eat,
10,085   then she bathed her.
Afterward she hid her under some old material.
Her belly was very big.

When he returned from hunting,
Jaguar placed the game in the usual place.
10,090   His aged mother got up.
She poured out water,
in the place where every day Jaguar took a bath.
Then she went off to cook.
Jaguar washed and dried himself and got dressed.
10,095   His mother served the meal.
He ate very fast
until he had eaten his fill.
He ran some water over his mouth and hands.
Then he cut up and salted all the game that was left.
10,100   He put it out to dry.
Then he got up
and went out to stroll in front of his house.[30]

Jaguar smelt a sweet smell, a smell of muskmelon.
"What is it here that smells of melon?"
10,105   he asked his mother.
"There's nothing here," she replied.

But Jaguar found the woman
and he killed her.

After eating her,
10,110   Jaguar spat out remains of food,
scraps that remained between his teeth.
Immediately they started to move.
"*Kuin! Kuin!*" They trailed on the ground and wept . . .

His aged mother picked them up.
10,115   She put them in cotton wool.
She gave them something to eat.

They were three boys.[31]
Jaguar's mother brought them up.
They grew up fast.
10,120   Soon they had small arrows
and they began killing lizards.
As soon as they were big enough,
Jaguar made them some metal arrows.
He then taught them to hunt and to shoot with a bow.
10,125   When the boys went off with him
they were supposed to drive out the deer and brockets
by shouting *"Kou! Kou! Kou!"*
and throwing stones.
They brought back home what they bagged
10,130   and there they cut it up and salted it
before hanging it up to dry.
Jaguar was fond of them.

Later on, Maleiwa
—the youngest of the three brothers,
10,135   the only one with supernatural powers[32]—
himself killed some game.
He gave it to Jaguar's mother,
and the young men fed on it.

It was then that they picked up a habit,
10,140   the habit of stealing melons from Old Dove.
Every day they secretly went and picked some,
even if they were not hunting nearby.

Old Dove noticed.
She had seen their footprints.
10,145   She hid in the garden and kept watch.
"Don't climb over the fence round my garden!
Napütaala! Remains of food!
Saaliipüna! Leftovers from death!"
she shouted when she saw them.

10,150   The next day the brothers came back.
Again the old woman insulted them.
"Hey, there are the ones who steal my crop.
Those whose mother was eaten by Jaguar."
"Repeat what you said or I'll kill you," said Maleiwa.
10,155   "Leftover from death! Remains of food!
That's what you are!
What I say is what you were before.
You were between the teeth of Kulirapata.

Your mother was eaten by Jaguar.
10,160 It was not I who ate her,
there's no reason for you to steal all my crop."
"Is what you say true?" asked Maleiwa.
"It is true; Jaguar ate your mother."

When Dove had related what had occurred,
10,165 Maleiwa burnt her eyelashes with cotton wool.

Dove's eyes are now without lashes.
"*To'uta tee! To'uta tee!* Oh, my eyelashes! my eyelashes!"
she sings since that time.

Maleiwa then decided to kill Jaguar's mother.

10,170 While hunting,
the boys suddenly stopped driving out the deer,
and they went back home.

When they arrived, Maleiwa shot an arrow at the old woman.
The young men cut her up into pieces.
10,175 They hid her head and put the rest on to cook.
Maleiwa took on the appearance of Jaguar's mother,
—he was still little
but he had supernatural powers.
He had white hair.
10,180 He spun cotton by rolling it against his thigh.

Jaguar returned from hunting.
"Why didn't they come and get what I'd bagged?"
he asked his mother.
"They came straight back
10,185 carrying what they had killed.
Eat! Eat!
He who is hungry should not worry his head."
It was Maleiwa saying this, in the mother's place,
with white hair, spinning cotton . . .
10,190 Ravenous, Jaguar leapt on the food.
After three mouthfuls, his teeth began to grind.
"*Poosh! Poosh! Shia pii! Shia pii!*
Poosh! Poosh! It's your mother! It's your mother!"
said the teeth.
10,195 Jaguar immediately spat out the meat on the ground.
He had understood.
He leapt at one of the young men.

Maleiwa immediately turned himself back into a boy.
He shot arrows at Jaguar

10,200   but without success.
Jaguar also shot arrows.
But neither of them could hit the other.

Near his home Jaguar made a stone wall.
Maleiwa tried to chase him away from it,
10,205   but Jaguar kept coming back.
Again they shot arrows at one another,
siwarai arrows, with metal tips.
They were equal.
The arrows did not hit them.

10,210   But Jaguar felt harried.
Soon he had to leave Jorolamatu,
where his mother's house was located.
Maleiwa set off in pursuit of him.
He shot his arrows on Iitujulu mountain
10,215   and on the nearby hills.
Jaguar fled, filled with terror.
Maleiwa would not let him sleep.
They were very far away
and still they went on running.

10,220   Maleiwa lighted fires
before and behind Jaguar.
But Jaguar got away.
He then arrived at the dwelling of the snail *julera*.[33]
"Help me, grandfather!
10,225   Give me something to drink! I'm dying of thirst!"
Jaguar was burnt all over.
Even today
the black fire marks can still be seen on his skin!
But the man had hidden his water.
10,230   It was Maleiwa who had asked him to do so.
"I'll give you a drink if you give me your arse."
"Am I not a man?" replied Jaguar.
"If you are a man, go away!" said Julera.
Jaguar offered him his arrows.
10,235   Julera had no use for them.
He offered him a poisoned arrow.
Julera refused it.
Maleiwa was about to arrive . . .
"Do what you will with me," said Jaguar.
10,240   Through his anus, Julera entered him, entered him . . .
Immediately afterward he hid in the Brazil tree,[34]
without giving Jaguar any water.

Furious, Jaguar clawed the bark of the tree
but he did not find Julera.
10,245 Since that day,
the Brazil tree is scored with deep scratches.
Jaguar started running again.
Soon he met Armadillo and asked him for water.
Maleiwa had asked Armadillo to do the same as Julera.
10,250 "I'll give you some water if you give me your arse."
"Take it," said Jaguar, who was very thirsty.
Armadillo skewered him, skewered him, skewered him . . .
But afterward he tried to go back home,
refusing to give Jaguar the water.
10,255 Jaguar then clawed his body
and cut off his head.

When Maleiwa arrived
he found Armadillo stretched out on the ground, dead.
Maleiwa shot down a *walusechi* bird.
10,260 He cut off his head
and he put it on Armadillo.
Since that time Armadillo has a scratched body
and a toothless mouth.
"What happened?" Maleiwa asked him.
10,265 Armadillo recounted what he had done.
"Good!
The jaguar will remain a pederast,"[35] said Maleiwa.

Maleiwa continued in pursuit of Jaguar
very far,
10,270 all the way to a mountain where he took refuge.[36] ⇌

There Jaguar had his home,
in a place where *palemasü* trees abounded.[37]
"What can I do against him?" Maleiwa wondered.

Maleiwa assumed the appearance of a woman.
10,275 He set off for Jaguar's abode,
to ask him for some *palemasü* fruits.
On her shoulder the woman carried a woven bag.
"I come in search of *palemasü* fruits," she said.
"Alas, they are not yet ripe.
10,280 But stay a while, I'll tell you a story,"
replied Jaguar.
"No, my child is waiting for me at home."
The woman wanted to go back there.

Jaguar caused a very violent rain to fall.

10,285 The woman had to go into a house,
a house that immediately turned into a stone.

Maleiwa was enclosed in the stone.
He then called all the ants.
They began digging.
10,290 "Here we are! We have hollowed out our little path,"
said Ant.
Maleiwa worked his way into it,
but in doing so he scraped himself.
His blood gushed out.

10,295 He then called the birds.
"Bathe in this blood,"
he said to the macaw, to the cardinal, to the troopial,
to all birds whose feathers are now marked with red.

"What shall I do?" Maleiwa then wondered.
10,300 He assumed the form of a woman who has just given birth.
Her breast could be seen, from which milk flowed.
"I would like some *palemasü* fruits."
"They are still green."
Maleiwa looked at them and they ripened immediately.
10,305 "Wait! I'll tell you a story," said Jaguar.
"No, my child is waiting for me.
He must already be crying."
Jaguar climbed up the tree to pick the fruit.
When he was very high
10,310 Maleiwa lifted his eyes toward it.
Under the effect of his gaze
the *palemasü* tree grew higher and higher and higher.

Maleiwa then struck the tree.
Its fruits were scattered all over the countryside.
10,315 and Jaguar fell very far away, in Lower Guajira.

Maleiwa abandoned him
in a desolate region where he remained jaguar.
A region so far away that today
jaguars never come any more to Upper Guajira. ⇌

10,320 Maleiwa then headed toward the sea.

He met a woman spinning cotton.
He wanted to touch her
and to caress her.
But the woman protested.
10,325 She threatened him.

He would have liked to lie with her.
"Leave me alone
or else I'll strike you!"
Maleiwa placed his hands on her.

10,330   "*Houu! Houuu! . . . Hou! . . .*
The woman was the sea.
She spread over the land,
and she tried to drown Maleiwa.
He fled before her.
10,335   But the sea continued to advance.
Maleiwa climbed to the top of the mountain Iitujulu.
The sea was still advancing.
It was about to submerge him . . .

But suddenly
10,340   the mountain Iitujulu rose.
It grew higher and higher.
Maleiwa climbed up it all the way to the top.
It had become a huge mountain.

The sea finally came to a halt, exhausted.
10,345   But it covered all the earth.

Maleiwa pondered.
He did not want to stay there.
He had with him arrows made of *koushot* wood.
He used them as a stick and pivot.
10,350   Rolling the stick between his palms and blowing.
Maleiwa made fire.
He gathered some wood and some smooth,
very hard black stones.
He threw them into the fire.

10,355   When the stones were hot,
he pushed one with his foot
in the direction of Upper Guajira, which was nearby.
He took a sling
and he sent the others further away,
10,360   one to the north,
one to the south,
one to the west . . .
"*Kaoo! Kaoo!*"
cried the fleeing sea.

10,365   The world reappeared.
The sea dried up.

It came to a halt there where the shore now is.
Near the top of the mountain Iitujulu
its trace can still be seen. ⇌

10,370 "What can I do now?" said Maleiwa.
He retraced his steps.
He went to Chimita, by the seashore,
where the soil is clayey,
where the rocks are covered with marks,
10,375 where the Guajiro now make pottery.
There he saw the tracks of cows, horses, dogs, . . .
He saw the tracks of Guajiros.
He then took some clay
and he began to make living beings.
10,380 He molded the earth
and with it he made kinds of cords.
He fashioned them and polished them with his hands.
With a snap of his fingers
he made birds.
10,385 With the help of Rain, Maleiwa made men.
"It is they who will speak," he said.
He also made branding irons
to distinguish each clan.
Then he made figurines that resembled cattle.

10,390 Among the clans he distributed people, animals, and things.
To the rich, Maleiwa distributed cheese and livestock.
"These animals will be yours," he told them.
But to the poor he gave only a long pole,
and made them take another path.
10,395 "With the pole you'll be able to eat dates,
and so you won't die of hunger."

Maleiwa also placed weapons in men's hands:
bows, arrows, rifles, machetes . . .
"This will be for killing people.
10,400 This will be for cutting up and preparing your food."
He gave them a spade.
"With this you will work for your wives,
your mothers, and your mothers-in-law. . . ." ⇌

But woman's vulva presented a serious defect.
10,405 It had teeth.
"*Kürülü! Kürülü! Kürülü!*"
the vulva said when men drew near.

Maleiwa thought that he would not have grandsons.

Men were frightened of mating.
10,410　Women were gradually dying.
"What would be a good thing to do?" he wondered.

Maleiwa went to Wotkasainru.
In that place was a girl named Tonkolu.[38]
She was swimming in cold, deep water.
10,415　Maleiwa went and bathed with her.
He could clearly see the large teeth of her vulva.
He heard them grinding together.
He was carrying with him his bow and arrows.
He drew near to the girl.
10,420　"*Too! Pots!*"
He struck her vulva with an arrow.
The teeth were at once turned into stones.
The girl got out of the water,
covered with blood.
10,425　She sat down on a stone.

That stone can still be seen, at Wotkasainru.
It is red with that blood,
surrounded by red stones, smaller ones. . . . ⇌

(These stories were recounted respectively by:
　Petronila Uliana [aged about thirty] and her father, Ramansita
Uliyu, living at Makalaitpao, in Colombian Guajira; recorded on
February 13, 1970, and July 17 and 18, 1973.
　Iisho Jayaliyu, alias Felipe Fernández; recorded on June 9, 1969.
　Shatui Uliyu, alias José del Carmen, living at Kasusain [Venezuela];
recorded on September 21, 1969.)

PART TWO
Analysis

1. Guajiro Oral Literature and Structural Analysis

To take the view that all myths follow the same pattern and that consequently a single key can unlock every one of them clearly reflects an unrealistic desire constantly to ignore differences and to reduce the many to the one; and here, to take shortcuts where none exist. (R. Caillois, *Le Mythe et l'homme* [Paris, 1938])

When on June 7, 1969, I first recorded a Guajiro tale, I was entering a virtually unexplored mythical universe. Up to that time no searching study had been made of the oral literature of the Guajiro.[1] I make this clear not in order to voice satisfaction at having filled a gap but because it is necessary to state briefly what my choices, limitations, and difficulties were when I came to deal with this unknown universe.

My primary concern was to identify, in regard to this Indian people whose ritual is very unobtrusive, not to say minimal, certain aspects of religious and philosophical thought that are usually and often quite rightly considered to be expressed in nonliterate societies spontaneously through mythology. But I soon discovered that the Guajiro did not invariably answer my pressing questions by recourse to myths. During my first investigation I was often disheartened by an impression of inconsistency created by the Indians' tales. Influenced by ethnological works that settled the problem of Guajiro oral literature by asserting that as a result of the "high degree of acculturation" of those Indians it no longer existed, I sometimes felt like an archaeologist uncovering the remains of a body of thought no longer true to itself. The myths collected seemed to be no more than the surviving traces of an architecture forever ruined.

The storytellers had faith in their stories, however, and their audience testified to the authenticity and importance of a large number of them. In this tangle of Guajiro oral literature, guiding principles soon emerged. As my knowledge of it grew, I was able to discern more clearly its general pattern.

When I asked them to recount traditional stories, men and women alike most readily proposed their songs.[2] Made up of a very large number of couplets between which the singers halt briefly to catch their breath, these songs can last several hours and thus constitute a real endurance test. Their subject matter is either anecdotal, or biographical or historical.[3] The themes most frequently heard include the pursuit of a desired woman, the praises of a sister or wife, the tale of a man killed fighting, an account of wars between clans. Despite the daunting length and limited interest of these songs,[4] I collected several dozen of them, if only to "hook" certain narrators who were anxious to interpret them before recounting any other tale, or to enable others who knew only those to experience the fascinating pleasure of hearing the recording of their voices. I also wished to be sure that, in omitting from my study this area of Guajiro oral literature, I was not overlooking a significant part of their mythical thought.

From the viewpoint adopted here, the songs of the shamans[5] also proved to be of little interest. I thought at first that they might contain profound messages on account of the privileged functions of those performing them. Always accompanied by the rhythmical shaking of the rattle, they are supposed to provide a commentary on the progression of the cure and, in particular, to give an account of the tribulations of the shaman's *spirits*. After recording ten or so such songs—by means of highly elaborate arrangements, since the shaman performs them only in the presence of the sick person and no one else—I had to face the fact that they did not, as an organized form of expression, possess any deep significance. In reality, they generally consist of a muttering punctuated by occasional intelligible words.

I then directed my efforts toward spoken tales.[6] As I collected more and more of them, I began to distinguish several major themes. Some of them allude to the cultural hero Maleiwa, creator of men and modifier of the world. Certain of their episodes recur in other forms in a great deal of Amerindian oral literature—among the Warao, the Kuna, the Makiritare, the Waiwai, the Mundukuru, the Tukano, and others. I was struck by the scant interest taken by the Guajiro in such tales. Few were familiar with them. The majority knew only their most striking episodes, and collecting them was sometimes like digging for the remains of a dead culture. When I spoke to them of Maleiwa, many fell silent. Some even said that we—the *alijunas*—should be better acquainted with his story than they. This lack of interest in Maleiwa surprised me, as all the works written about the Guajiro had assigned the utmost importance to him. But by the end of my investigation I was convinced that his preeminence reflected the inadequacy or the strongly slanted character of these previous studies. Today Maleiwa is of little importance to the Guajiro.[7]

At the same time I discovered other tales that, on the contrary, gave continual proof of their current relevance. These captured my interest, and I sought them out with the greatest persistence. They involve Pulowi, Juya, *wanülüs, yolujas,* and all the supernatural beings that have a real existence for the Guajiro, since they are at the origin of daily concerns and torments. They tell of sickness, death, the beyond, and other things. The Guajiro always feel very concerned by this kind of tale. Some, acknowledging more readily than others the power of the spoken word, even avoid relating such tales for fear of bringing bad dreams and misfortune upon themselves or, when they do recount them, assume a grave or circumspect attitude. These tales are listened to at times with a mixture of fear and respect. They are related in a confidential tone to a limited audience.

Another group of tales deals with domestic animals—horses, cows, goats, and sheep—that were introduced in colonial times and now have an essential place in Guajiro life. These tales are of considerable interest for they are able to shed light on the way in which a myth is developed or transformed. For this reason I made a point of collecting and studying them as well.

The Guajiro also have a great liking for funny stories. Some have a definite etiological significance; with great subtlety and invention they tell, for instance, how the fox or the dog got its tail, why the tortoise's shell is covered in cracks, why the bittern has twisted feet. They constitute a magnificent bestiary and bear witness to an extraordinary faculty of observation and analysis. Others tend to be on the bawdy side and often serve to provoke women.

Does this represent the whole of Guajiro oral literature? Did I meet the true custodians of mythological knowledge? I can now say yes, after spending two long periods in the field and recording more than four hundred tales in the most varied regions of the peninsula.[8]

Among the Guajiro there are no "specialists" in religious matters. Although the shamans often give evidence of considerable intellectual curiosity and possess greater knowledge of mythology than the ordinary people, they have only an indirect influence on Guajiro spiritual life. In this culture there are no initiation rites or secret societies. No allusion is ever made to a profound type of knowledge as opposed to a superficial type, accessible only to an elite.

Nor are there any professional storytellers. A large number of individuals, men and women alike, derive real pleasure from storytelling and do so with much talent. Those whom I met were either elderly Indians reputed for their skill in storytelling and for knowing a large number of tales—one of them recounted some thirty to me—or occasional narrators who knew two or three. I thus heard about fifty storytellers, including six shamans.

The Guajiro generally relate their stories in a straightforward manner without any particular solemnity. Often men gather to drink, talk, and tell stories. In the course of traveling about together, at gatherings on the occasion of a celebration, a dance, or a burial, it is not uncommon for a group to form around two or three storytellers. The gatherings at

which I was present and of which I was often the cause were joyful occasions for the men and women who came together. Children always
came along, fascinated. But usually, far from ending in a mood of hap-
piness, they would finish with words uttered in confidence or with the
anguished recollection of the unavoidable dangers of death presented by
certain supernatural beings. Each then communicated his or her own
experience or recounted as proof what he or she had undergone or what
had happened to a close relation. For the Indians it was as it were an
opportunity to confirm their beliefs.

The following analysis is governed by a number of rules and principles designed to ensure its effectiveness while defining its limits.

Above all, it is inward-looking. By this I mean that it is centered exclusively on the Guajiro universe. Although a number of the tales reveal
through some of their episodes that they form part of a pan-American
mythical complex, I have abstained here from any comparative study
involving myths belonging to other Indian groups. Nor have I concerned
myself with whether the mechanisms of Guajiro mythical thought that
I have pinpointed obey universal rules. Nor do I think that I have suc-
cumbed to the temptation of filling at all costs the boxes of a preconceived model by dint of roundabout methods, subtleties, or fine distinc-
tions derived from our own cultural codes. I have taken the view that
Guajiro oral literature has been shaped primarily by the place and way
of life of the people who have persisted in transmitting it from generation to generation, and that it has shaped them in return. This is why I
have studied the myths in themselves, but whenever possible I have also
drawn attention to the relations between those myths and the life of the
people who recount them.

This rejection of any a priori formalization makes it necessary to
identify the subject more specifically and more finely. It calls for a
study in depth of other levels of the culture in relation to the oral literature, concomitant with the collecting of that literature, and it also
makes it desirable to arrive at classifications and categories peculiar to
that culture. It leads to the discovery of areas hitherto unnoticed or
very inadequately studied, which can be assumed to have given sub-
stance to the mythology or to be clear applications thereof.

Furthermore, this analysis covers only a portion of the tales and information collected in the course of fourteen months of field research.
It by no means claims to be a key to the whole of Guajiro oral literature
and ritual. I subscribe to the principle that at least part of the complex
formed by Guajiro mythology and society constitutes a system endowed with some degree of coherence. The aim of this study is to reveal
that coherence and to define its nature.

The boundaries of the analysis became apparent as the work proceeded. The selection made among the ethnographic materials is in no case the result of a distribution among preconceived and hence highly arbitrary classes. It was guided solely by the choice of the reference point around which it was centered: the myth that I decided to call—departing in this one case from my "rule of inwardness"—"The Journey to the Beyond: A Guajiro Eurydice." This myth was chosen because it belonged to that part of the mythology which, at the end of my first investigation, had appeared the most topical and hence most susceptible of coherence—a quality that, in the light of a rapid and superficial review of the data collected, should be denied it but that, as a result of long contact with the Indians, I intuitively felt it possessed. This reference myth provided a point of anchorage for all the other tales and all the other facts belonging in some way to the system gradually brought to light.

I have openly used certain tools and principles peculiar to what is known as structural analysis, and I acknowledge my debt to Claude Lévi-Strauss. But deliberately ignoring the ideological quarrels that have developed around what for some has become a dogma, I have used the structuralist approach in the context of fieldwork. It is unquestionably effective in such work, which has now become essential. It is my hope that this study affords proof of this.

But the results obtained should by no means be regarded as irrefutable or final. The analysis stops at a point where, if it had been continued, it would have become purely conjectural, detached from all reality or ethnographic proof. It made and will continue to make it possible to establish models, sets of possible circumstances, on the basis of which it is permitted to ask questions, raise problems, and even to foresee certain situations. But it goes without saying that these developments may be called into question by the very facts whose discovery they will have made possible, on account of that inevitable incompleteness of ethnological research in which any claim to exhaustiveness is but an impossible dream. Only the systematic alternation of ethnographical exploration and ethnological synthesis can lead to a more and more finely tuned approach to reality and contribute to the formulation of better-adapted theories.

2. Juya and Pulowi

It is true that the decoding of a myth must be keyed to its
sequential pattern . . . but the goal, perhaps a fundamental one,
is to break up the mythical tale in order to detect its primary
elements, which should themselves be set in parallel with those
offered by other versions of the same myth or by different groups
of legends. The initial tale, far from being closed in upon itself in
such a way as to form, as a totality, a unique work, opens out on
the contrary, in each of its sequences, upon all the other texts
that put into effect the same code system, the keys to which need
to be discovered. In this sense, for the mythologist, all myths, be
they elaborate or rudimentary, are situated at the same level and
have, from the heuristic standpoint, the same value.

(J. P. Vernant and P. Vidal-Naquet,
Mythe et tragédie en Grèce ancienne [Paris, 1972], pp. 7–8)

Feeling intuitively that Pulowi was a key concept in Guajiro religious
thought, I put together all the tales featuring this mythical figure along
with those involving Juya, her husband. Then other narratives were
added as I discovered that they contained references to beings, acts, or
things that, through various links, were directly related to this nucleus
of tales. When this work was done I found myself with a set of some two
hundred tales of varying length and significance. Reading through them
I was struck first by the fact that certain qualities were always associated with Pulowi, while Juya was invested with exactly the opposite
attributes. A system thus emerged, made up of two classes. To each element in one corresponds an element in the other that is always, according to a particular Guajiro standpoint, its contrary. These pairs of opposite elements define what, for the sake of convenience, I have chosen
to call the categories or dimensions of Guajiro mythical thought.

Knowledge of these categories and of their symbolic expressions
allows us, in fact, to gain insight into a large number of myths, rites,
and beliefs. Such knowledge reveals to us a meaning that is far from
immediately apparent, since it applies to a domain where beings and
things serve as metaphors for a highly symbolic mode of thinking that
always appears to be directed toward the greatest possible degree of
coherence.

In this chapter we shall see that the pair formed by Juya and Pulowi
and, incidentally, the figure and concept of *wanülü*, seem to have been
devised to reveal a system of fundamental oppositions and to synthesize
it. From the outset I request the reader's indulgence. Tiresome as this

technical analysis may seem, it provides information about the culture and representations of the Guajiro that will prove necessary for the development of the following chapter.

THE MEANINGS OF WORDS

First of all the extensive semantic connotations of the three Indian words *juya, pulowi,* and *wanülü* must be defined.

In Guajiro, the word *juya,* when treated as a feminine substantive, first denotes the rain, in the sense of a meteorological phenomenon. Thus, *eittasü juyakat* means "the rain is falling"[1] and *ememejasü wane juya* means "a fine rain is falling."[2]

In a more restrictive sense, *juya* signifies the main wet season, the October rains. It is then opposed to *Iiwa,* the short wet season, the May rains.[3] But in this sense many Guajiro tend more readily to use the derivative *juyapü* (*juyapu* or *juyamülatü*). They will say, for instance, *maima süttia wayu juyapü:* "The Guajiro have plentiful crops during the main rainy season." In Guajiro thought *juyapü* is clearly opposed to *jouktaleu,* or *jouktai-jamü,* the "long dry season."

In an even narrower sense *juya* designates, among the rains of the main wet season, those associated with *juyo'u,* the star Arcturus. These rains occur during the period when the star disappears on the western horizon just after sunset. This corresponds to the first days of October and generally coincides with the period of maximum rainfall. *Juya* is then opposed to the other rains of the wet season, associated with other stars, following the same principle that links *juyo'u* with *juya.* In most cases the context affords an adequate indication of the sense in which the speaker is using the word *juya* (a list of the Guajiro seasons and their associated stars is given in chapter 4).

Juya also signifies the year, which is the largest Guajiro unit of time. It is equal to the period of a stellar cycle. A new year begins when Arcturus becomes invisible. Mention may also be made here of the word *auyase* (or *ouyase*), "age," which derives directly from *juya.*[4]

Finally, *Juya* is the name given to the mythical male figure who is regarded by the Guajiro primarily as the master of the rain, but he is also endowed with many other characteristics, which this study seeks to identify. In this case, of course, the word is always treated as masculine.

This polysemia of the word *juya* has important consequences, as two examples will suffice to show. The word *juyo'u,* signifying the star Arcturus, is formed of the monemes *juya* and *o'u.* The latter means "eye" (of man or of animal) or "hole, orifice."[5] *Juyo'u* may therefore be taken to mean the "eye of Juya," or the "hole of the rain." Some Guajiro are aware of this dual etymology and of the resulting ambiguity. Their explanation for the second meaning is that the hole referred to is that represented by the star Arcturus, through which emerges the rain that falls in the first days of October.[6] However, the first of these etymologies is the one most commonly offered, for it is associated with a more complete representation of the mythical figure in the night sky. Indeed, if Arcturus is his eye, two constellations, known as *stüna juya*,[7] represent his arms. One points to the north and runs from Arcturus to the Great Bear. It includes ε, γ, and λ of the Waggoner and η, ζ, ε, δ, α, β, and γ of the Great Bear. The other, running southward, is plotted much more hazily. It would seem to link Arcturus to the Southern Cross, passing through Virgo and Centaurus.[8]

The two ways in which the Guajiro speak of and hence interpret certain atmospheric phenomena linked to the rain will serve as a second example. Thus, "it is raining" is expressed either by *shiittüin juya* or by *niittüin juya*. The first expression, treated as feminine, may be rendered literally as "(the) rain falls to the ground." The second, in the masculine, may be translated as "Juya (Rain) shoots," implying "as does a hunter." Likewise, to express the idea of lightning, there is the expression *nükapüla juya*, "Juya's weapon" (from *aapüla*, "weapon"), or *sükapüla juya*, "the rain's weapon." Thunder is referred to as *nütürüla juya*, "Juya's rumbling," or *sütürüla juya*, "the muffled, rumbling noise of the rain." To express this idea there also exist, in place of these nominal forms, the verbal forms *nütüttatüin juya* or *sütüttatüin juya*, which can be rendered respectively by "Juya roars" or "the rain thunders." In ordinary conversation the two forms, masculine and feminine, can both be used. But those who are familiar with the myths and recount them readily use the more suggestive masculine form, since to the concrete meaning it adds a symbolic dimension.[9]

It is also noteworthy that from the word *juya* derives the verbal form *kouyashawa*, "to have rain, to be a place where it rains." Thus *kouyashechikai pia* means "you will be the one who has rain." *Kouyashechikai sulu tü numainja*, literally "he has rains in his lands," may be rendered by "in his lands it rains a great deal." There also exist the personal forms *touyasü, puuyasü* . . . , which should be rendered literally by "I have rained, you have rained . . ."! They generally relate to Juya. (This example suggests some of the difficulties involved in the translation of myths.)

The Guajiro designate by the name *pulowi*[10] places they consider to be dangerous, places they keep away from so as not to vanish there forever or fall seriously ill. The *pulowis* are reputed to swallow human beings or their domestic animals. Supernatural beings may appear in their vicinity—men or animals with evil intentions. The *pulowis* are usually situated on small hills or in areas of dense vegetation. They are often indicated by stretches of stagnant water or by holes or openings in the ground or in rocks. They are sometimes reputed to be the source of muffled, drawn-out noises, vibrations, or shakings of the ground, "noises and whistlings seeming to emanate from countless animals," as the Indians say. Existing in great number and distributed over the entire Indian territory, the *pulowis* are always on the edges of areas inhabited by humans, in places that can be reached fairly easily by people and domestic animals. There are none on the peaks of the high, rugged mountains of Guajira, which are difficult of access and generally at a distance from any inhabited place.[11] When it is understood in this sense, bilingual Indians generally translate the word *pulowi* by the Spanish word *volcán* (English *volcano*).

Pulowi[12] also designates the female mythical being named over and over again in the first part of this work. Her many qualities, like those of her husband, Juya, are the subject of the following study.

Finally, the word *pulowi* is used as an epithet. It will be said, for instance, that *pulowikaya tü jirunukot*, "the shooting star is *pulowi*," or *pulowi tü majayülü*, "that young woman is *pulowi*." Let us say provisionally that it describes then a phenomenon or a being that "represents" or carries within itself the *pulowi* "principle" and acts, so to speak, as its emissary.[13]

Pulowi derives from the verb *püla*, and in all its meanings this relationship is implicitly felt. According to its context *püla* can be translated by "to have supernatural powers," "to be dangerous," "to be ill-willed," "to be forbidden," "to be taboo," or "to be learned."[14] Directly related to these words is the term *pülaiwa*, by means of which it is possible to express simultaneously the idea of a unified, active, as it were emerging world and that encompassed by the term *pulowi*.[15] From *püla* also derive the verbs *apülaja* and *apülajawa*, "to forbid, to abstain" (generally on account of medical instructions), or "to be transformed, to change appearance."[16] Another important notion is expressed by the verb *kapülainwa*, or *apülainwa*, which can be translated by "to be contagious, to be contaminated." A whole set of diseases afflicting mainly children and pregnant women fall into the category *süpülainwa uchi*,[17] literally "contagion through animals." These are said to be caused by the ingestion of food that has been in contact with animals called *kapülainsü*[18] or simply through touching objects that they are assumed to have brushed against. From *püla* also stem the verbs *püla a'in* and *apülajawa a'in*, which can be translated, respectively, "to be pretentious," in the sense of not wishing to do like others, to want to stand out, and "to be proud, to be puffed up with vanity." From these comes the very important notion of *pülainrü*, designating young women who take pleasure in seclusion[19] and want at all costs to prolong it, refusing to receive any suitors, even the most prestigious ones.[20]

The word *wanülü* has three principal meanings.

Used in the feminine, it denotes a distressing or serious illness necessitating the shaman's intervention, as opposed to *ayule* (or *ayulia*), the first stage or a mild illness cured by drugs, massages, or ignipuncture.[21] The illnesses clearly placed in this category include those known as *süpülainwa*, referred to above, as well as the disease *pulowisira*, occasioned by indirect contact with *pulowi* places or beings, and more generally that called *kalia* or *oustawa*,[22] resulting from aggression by supernatural beings, especially *wanülus*.

Used in the masculine, *wanülü* designates that supernatural being referred to earlier in the tales who can assume a variety of human appearances: a Guajiro dressed in black, an *alijuna*, that is, a white person, dressed in shining bright or dark clothes, a man of normal aspect but odd behavior, completely silent or, on the contrary, making strange and powerful whistling noises. However, the *wanülü's* appearance often so closely resembles that of humans that he cannot be recognized immediately but only later, when the effects of an encounter with him are beginning to be felt. For he shoots invisible arrows at the Guajiro, mortally wounding them or doing them serious injury. On returning home the victim, who typically presents such symptoms as internal hemorrhaging accompanied by vomiting of blood and violent chest or stomach pains, will search his or her memory for signs of an encounter with a being who might personify *wanülü*. The victim will then offer hypotheses, but only the shaman hurriedly called in has the knowledge needed to make the diagnosis. "*Shia nütkaka wanülükai tia, wanülü kevirakai!*" the shaman will say, for instance: "He has had an arrow shot into him by the *wanülü*, the whistling *wanülü*." The *wanülüs* operate by night, at dawn or dusk. They prefer to attack those who are away from their homes, hunters setting out or returning, women going to a distant well for water, those who travel at night to arrive at the market the next morning (see Part One, lines 2068–6024). According to a large number of Guajiros they dwell in *pulowi* places.

Some shamans apparently understand the word *wanülü* in an entirely different way. In their view it is synonymous with the idea of *asheyu* or *ajuna*,[23] translated in the preceding tales as the shaman's "spirit." Briefly, the *asheyu* is an immaterial entity, spirit, soul, or power possessed only by shamans[24] (and sometimes diviners), with which they are able to communicate. From it they receive information about sickness and how to cure it; in return, the shamans are reputed to give the *asheyu* material goods of which they are the custodians and the sick person and his kin the providers. When the shamans employ the word *wanülü* to express this idea of *spirit*, their formulations may become very ambiguous, since in their mouths the same word can have the three meanings referred to here.[25] But at the same time the ambiguity resulting from the polysemia of the word *wanülü* makes it symbolically very rich.[26] However, in order to make their account of the progression of the cure intelligible to an audience not used to the subtleties of their thinking or eager for details (as are a few acculturated Guajiros and ethnographers!), the shamans often add to the word *wanülü* an epithet when it is meant in the sense of *spirit*. Thus they may speak of *wanülü anashikai*, the "good *wanülü*," or *wanülü washiru*, the "rich *wanülü*"—in contrast with *wanülü jashichi*, the "fierce *wanülü*," who shoots arrows and kills—or *wanülü taseyukai*, "the *wanülü* who is our *spirit*," or *wanülü tajunakai*, "the *wanülü* over us."[27]

TWO OPPOSING BEINGS

A selective review of Guajiro myths and tales, together with certain ethnographic observations, should now make it possible to identify the highly marked and clearly opposing characteristics presented by each of the partners in the couple formed by Juya and Pulowi.

Man and Woman

Juya is described above all as a masculine and, one might even say, a hypermasculine figure. For he epitomizes all the qualities that for the Guajiro characterize a real man, a he-man, a *tolo*. He manages to seduce *pülainrü* girls and to make them his wives. This prodigious begetter can even give them children although they always remain in seclusion (see Part One, lines 535–539). In this respect the Guajiro compare him with Kashi, Moon, about whom they say, "He is our father, he is the one who possesses all women" (cf. lines 9009–9015). Juya is also the most powerful hunter and warrior: "He possesses a weapon (*kapülashi*) of matchless force and accuracy," say the Guajiro. His weapon is lightning (*nükapüla juya*); a very popular myth that I shall not quote here relates how Juya, whose extraordinary power is magnified, stole it from Ala'ala, the Howler Monkey, because he used it indiscriminately. We saw in the brief linguistic notes that open this chapter how this relationship between Juya and hunting is emphasized by the language. It may be recalled, for instance, that "there is lightning" is expressed literally as "Juya shoots": he shoots with lightning just as the Guajiro hunters shoot with their arrows or their firearms. And, just like wars between clans, hunting is regarded by the Guajiro as the male activity par excellence. Although of minor importance today from the economic standpoint, it has for that reason continued to enjoy great prestige (see below, "On the Side of the Animals . . .").[28]

Pulowi, on the contrary, is hyperfeminine. To her are assigned those dark and fatal powers that Guajiro men associate with "real women," *jierü*. She abducts men, often overskillful hunters or fishermen—in other words the most virile men—in order to draw them into her subterranean world and possess them completely by barring them forever from the world of the living (see Part One, lines 843–2067). Her sex organ is reputed to have a fatal power: one look at it can bring death (lines 419–428).[29]

The Mobile and the Fixed; the Unique and the Manifold

Juya is mobile (*kakuashi*) and unique (*wane*). He is seen traveling all over Guajiro territory to abduct a young woman, to rain here and there, or to come to the rescue of his daughters in danger (see lines 616–638, 9022–10,007). But he moves so fast that he can give the impression of being everywhere at the same time. He never stays long in the same place, just like the rains that, on the peninsula of Guajira, are always violent and of brief duration, stormy and confined to one spot.[30]

Pulowi is fixed (*jimatsü*) and manifold (*maima*). The *pulowi* places where she dwells are distributed throughout Guajira, and there are several in each inhabited area. In each of the five regions in which my ethnographic investigations were conducted I counted between one and three "present-day" *pulowi* places.[31] *Pulowi* places are precisely located and a proper name is attributed to them. Thus through the myths were known those of Ayajui, Yaulama, Matujai, and Ouysimalu (lines 534–657, 666–689, 884–928, and 940–2067, respectively). There are also *pulowi* places in the sea (line 720). These are of course not strictly localized and usually not named, except for a few localities on the coast or certain reefs designated by the generic expression *pala puloina*, "*pulowi* sea." Noisy with the beating of the waves and the breakers crashing down, in the view of the Guajiro they attest to Pulowi's presence. For there is no doubt in the minds of the Indians that in each *pulowi* place Pulowi exists, since at any time she can reveal herself there.

This assertion would, at first sight, seem to be contradicted by the story "Pulowi of the Land and Pulowi of the Sea" (lines 718–842). For, interpreted literally, it would suggest that there exist two Pulowis, one living in the earth and the other reigning under the sea. In fact, in this myth each of these figures represents respectively all the Pulowis of the land and all the Pulowis of the sea. They may be said to personify the land and the sea. This is confirmed by other versions in which, instead of calling them Pulowi of the land and Pulowi of the sea, the storytellers call them simply *Ma* and *Pala*, "Land" and "Sea," or, more vividly, *sa'in-ma* and *sa'in tü palakat*, literally "heart (or *soul*) of the land" and "heart (or *soul*) of the sea." On the one hand, then, the myth asserts that Pulowi is associated with the land and the sea alike. She is, so to speak, the living principle of both. Like her, both are deep, inaccessible, dangerous, and also indispensable, since they provide food.

But, on the other hand, the myth emphasizes that, from one angle, land and sea are in opposition to one another. In this it reflects and establishes the validity of the secondary oppositions that the Guajiro commonly establish between the animals of the land and the animals of the sea, between the life of the inland Indians and the life of those living by the shore, between hunting and fishing.

Above and Below

The Guajiro generally say that Juya dwells "very high up above the ground," *ipünapüna molu'u*. This is borne out by the myths: to return from his abode one must come down. It is by winding off her thread that Spider enables the "Guajiro Orpheus" to descend to earth after his long sojourn in Juya's world (lines 475–479); in another version Calabash, acting as his mount, makes him come back down to earth (see below, p. 117). In most of the variants of this myth, it is the birds who lead the hero from the "island" of Jepira to the "land of Juya" (e.g., below, p. 113). It is Dragonfly who notifies Juya of his daughters' misfortune (lines 603–618). It will be recalled that after abducting a young woman Juya rose up with her in the direction of the clouds (lines 9087–10,007).

Pulowi, on the contrary, is subterranean or submarine.[32] To reach her abode it is necessary to go down through hollows, natural openings in the earth, rock cavities, and chaos (cf. lines 1038–1039, 2036–2037). One plunges right into the deepest part of the trees and never comes out again:

> The deer came near a *toluich* tree,
> dense and impenetrable.
> He plunged into it.
> The Guajiro followed his tracks.
> He also went in under the *toluich* tree
> and he was swallowed up.
> He found himself in Pulowi's domain.
>
> (Extract from a tale by Saalachon Aapshana)

A variant of the myth "The Pulowi of Ayajui and the Daughters of Juya" relates that "Juya had to penetrate into the holes of Ayajui, all the way to the middle of the earth"[33] in order to wrest his daughters from Pulowi. Pulowi dwells "beneath the ground where people live." If the latter draw too close to the places from which she emerges, they are swallowed, engulfed, buried (cf. lines 686–689).[34] Similarly, Pulowi of the sea inhabits places beneath the water. Turtles or large rays lead fishermen away toward "her world" (cf. lines 870–874).[35]

Uniformity and Diversity of Appearances

The opposition between unique and manifold is reflected in the ways in which Juya and Pulowi reveal themselves to human beings.

Juya generally appears in the form of an ordinary Indian. This seems so self-evident that most of the time the storytellers neglect to mention it. Otherwise, lightning or rain, his essential attributes, suffice to express his presence (as in line 560). It will be seen later on that an *anolis*, a dragonfly, and a few other living beings may announce or signify his presence or act as intermediaries between him and humans. But they do not, strictly speaking, represent him.

Pulowi, however, if she is not the immobile woman of provocative appearance who is surprised in her house, reveals herself only through the most varied intermediaries or emissaries. Subterranean and mysterious, she is not confined to a fixed form. She is recognized essentially by her effects or through the behavior of her substitutes. In the course of a tale a Guajiro listener will immediately recognize a reference to a being or an action directly related to Pulowi and will comment, "*pulowi tia*," "that is *pulowi*." The traditional forms in which Pulowi usually reveals herself are extremely numerous. I shall not attempt here to draw up an exhaustive list of them but shall merely refer to the main ones and, in particular, give evidence of their "associations" with Pulowi.

Pulowi often assumes the features of a tantalizing Guajiro girl, exercising an irresistible attraction over men (lines 889–900). She also appears sometimes as a "foreign woman," an *alijuna*. Such, for instance, was the guise in which she came to an overfortunate fisherman, long after she had decided to inflict famine upon him:

> Long had he been unable to find anything . . .
> One morning he set out very early, before dawn.
> In his boat he found an *alijuna*,
> a young woman sitting down.
> "How are you? What do you need?"
> she asked him.
> "I am hungry and my children are hungry,
> I have long been unable to find any food," he said.
> "Come with me! Let's go from here!"
> The Guajiro went off with her, very far.

> It was not an *alijuna*.
> She was *pulowi* . . .

> (Extract from a tale by Samuerü Jayaliyuu, October 1969)

In this female form Pulowi can also appear to women, but far less often. An old Indian woman related the following to me: "One day I was taking my sheep out to graze. I was near the sea, in that *pulowi* place called Mojuai.[36] Suddenly, in the waves, I saw a woman advancing toward me with naked breasts. She emerged regularly from the water as turtles do . . . until she was so close to me that I ran away leaving my sheep. That woman was *pulowi*."

If need be, she assumes the appearance of a man. Such is true at least of the Pulowi of Ayajui (lines 581–585), and the Pulowi of Mashierü,[37] described as follows by an old Indian: "She looks like an *alijuna*, riding a mule. He is very wily. When you see him, he is always behind you. He has killed countless Guajiros. He who wants to die has only to go at night near that *pulowi* land. Next morning he will be as though drunk and will soon die."

Pulowi has immense power over game animals and, according to some, can even take on their form. Whatever the case, she knows how to use them as bait in order to lure hunters and fishermen into her lands. This role is most commonly played by deer, brockets, marine turtles, and large rays (see, for example, lines 870–874, 1002–1041). But sometimes the role of Pulowi's emissary is performed by young animals—often birds or small mammals—who are adopted and tamed by the Guajiro, usually by young women. One day they flee to the *pulowi* place from which they originate, pursued by their tearful protectors, who will vanish forever. Here, for instance, is the ending of the story of a young woman who had made a small squirrel into her pet. She fed him, slept with him, looked after him "like a son," until one day, having become full-grown, he vanished:

She followed his tracks.
She plunged into the bush, crossed a mountain . . .
She then met a young woman.
"Where do you come from?" she asked her.
"I come from my home, a long way away.
I am looking for my pet.
He's a little squirrel, he has got lost.
I am very grieved!" replied the young Guajiro woman.
The woman immediately turned into Pulowi.[38]
In a moment she gulped down the girl.
She locked her up in a house beneath the earth.
Thus she swallowed her down forever.

(Extract from a tale by "Wawai" Jayaliyuu, June 1969)

The Guajiro relate that Pulowi can transform herself into a reptile. She frequently takes the form of a "very big snake," of a huge *sarulu* boa, or of a *kasiwanau* boa[39] at the very moment when she swallows the Guajiro (lines 592–602). But some assert that she can take on this appearance permanently. Here is how, in August 1973, one man described a *pulowi* situated in the vicinity of Uribia, in Colombian Guajira:

She is a huge boa, far bigger than a cow.
She calls out like a deer.
Her head is bigger than a bull's head.
Some claim that she has horns.
But all who have seen her are dead.
One day two hunters decided to kill her.
They struck her with metal-tipped arrows.
A very strong fetid gas came out of her belly.
Two days later
the two men started to vomit blood.
They died soon after.
The snake still lives over there,
in that very *pulowi* land . . .

It is always said that reptiles abound in *pulowi* places, to such an extent that for the Guajiro "snake"[40] can signify "presence of *pulowi*." It then truly becomes its "metaphorical equivalent."

But the principal and most dangerous of Pulowi's emissaries is the *wanülü*, that supernatural being who was discussed at length at the beginning of this chapter. The Guajiro claim that Pulowi and Wanülü belong to the same family.[41] There are many who consider Wanülü to be Pulowi's brother or maternal uncle (lines 2069–2070). For the Guajiro this means that he is the male and hence mobile representative of the Pulowi matrilinear clan. In fact, he is the mobile substitute for Pulowi. Like her, the *wanülü* readily appears to overeager and overfortunate hunters, and in some tales he is even regarded as well as a "master of game animals."[42] Like Pulowi, he operates at night. Unmasked or fought by humans, he generally assumes the appearance of one of the reptiles, which are closely associated with Pulowi (lines 3004–3011, 4006–4049, 5083–6015).

Finally, a large variety of supernatural beings emanate from Pulowi and reveal her presence.[43] So it is with the *akalakuis* (or *akalapüis*), the *keralias*, the *wanesatais*, the *kojus*, the *josüs*, and, to some extent, the *epeyüis*.

Here follows a striking description of the first group:

The *akalapüis* dwell within the earth
and the earth where they live is *pulowi*.
They are the size of small children,
they go around in gangs.
They are always many, very many.
"*Shirivi! Shirivi!*" they whistle continuously.
It matters little whether he who meets them runs away.
The *akalapüis* always catch up with him.
They seize his mount.

They all grab hold of him.
Some climb up behind, others in front,
some this way, others that way.
Some seize his leg, others his arm . . .
The *akalapüis* make him fall to the ground.
They pull out his tongue
and he can never speak again.
They penetrate him through his anus,
they put their sex organs in all his orifices,
in his nostrils, in his ears, under his arms . . .
"*Shirivi! Shirivi! Shirivi!*"
they whistle as they abandon him,
before going back into the earth,
into their territory which is *pulowi* . . .

When, some time later,
people set out in search of the Guajiro,
they find him dead, killed by the *akalapüis*.
He died of that sickness called *pulowisira*,
for the *akalapüis* are *pulowi*.

(Recounted by Sepana Epieyu, alias Josefana Gonzales, on September 9,
1969. Aged about eighty, she lives at Aulejemerai, in Venezuelan Guajira.)

Some Guajiros assert that the *akalapüis* never attack women. In point
of fact, they live in steeply sloping areas that only men come near.
Others say that they resemble snakes and, like them, "race by, accompanied by wind."

The *keralias* behave in a similar way, with the difference that they
send out light and are the size of a normal man. They generally act
alone and commonly turn into reptiles. Consequently, they are often
placed in the category *wanülü* and are referred to as *wanülü keralia*.

The *keralia* can do many things.
He can turn into a boa,
he can turn into a rattlesnake,
he can turn into a *kasiwanau* snake.
Often he turns into an iguana . . .

He pursues people.
He clings to the tail of their mounts.
He makes them fall.
He uses their anus like a vagina.
He penetrates it with his sex organ.
People then fall sick.
They vomit blood,
they urinate blood,

they defecate blood.
And they die . . .

The *keralia*'s urine is very dangerous.
He who passes by at night
where the *keralia* stopped to urinate,
he falls seriously ill
with a sickness that few shamans can cure . . .

(Story by Majayule Jayaliyu, recounted on August 3, 1973. This woman, about fifty years old, is a shaman at Wüinkua in Venezuelan Guajira.)

Wanesatai, or *wanetünai*, literally "one-limb" or "one-leg," is a figure human in appearance but with only one leg, the foot of which is turned round the wrong way, or, other Guajiros say, with just one half of the body. He is often described riding a *shanatainrü*, a supernatural animal "who slightly resembles a mule but who moves extremely fast." Considered to be Pulowi's brother, Wanesatai is, however, deemed to be less dangerous than her other supernatural emissaries. Some tales even recount how he has been defeated by exceptionally strong men. One of his characteristics is that he does not attack people directly but requests tobacco from them in exchange for plants that give to those who consume them extraordinary physical agility. It is during such encounters that he can draw them toward Pulowi for whom he acts so to speak as a beater. The Guajiro who recognize him in time are able to avoid his trap and to keep the precious magical plants for themselves.

The *kojus*, who are far less well known, are said to frequent certain *pulowi* mountains in the Sierra Makuira, in the northeast of the Guajira peninsula. Like the *josüs*,[44] they are reputed to specialize in the extraction of people's tongues, thereby leaving them dumb. According to some, the *kojus*, of human appearance but heavily bearded, are capable of "killing with one blow people dreaming."

Finally, the Guajiro closely associate Epeyüi, the supernatural jaguar (Chapter 2, note 29), with Pulowi. Like her, "he is the earth," they say.[45] Like her, he appears to overeager hunters whose dogs he devours before attacking them. Impervious to their arrows, he inflicts scratches that cannot be healed. He is often held responsible for epidemics. In some traditional tales, he even personifies the epidemic: in a human form he travels all over Guajira spreading disease. The Indians speak of the threat he presents when they come together, on the occasion of *yonna* dances or "games of the goat," for instance, and it is sometimes said that an *epeyüi*[46] is one of the forms in which a *wanülü* appears.[47]

Rain and Drought

Juya is the rain. He personifies it. The rain is his power. He is "the one who rains." This was shown in detail at the beginning of this chapter.

Pulowi, on the contrary, is explicitly associated with drought (*jula*) and the dry season, *jouktale'u* (lines 7008–8019). She is linked with the rainbow; through it, or even directly, she opposes Juya and tries to prevent him from raining (lines 8020–8028). While, for the Guajiro, the rain comes from the sky, drought originates from the earth, hence essentially from Pulowi. In *pulowi* places there is always a great deal of wind, and the wind (*jouktai*), an emanation of the earth, is rightly considered by the Guajiro to be responsible for the dehydration of the soil. All Pulowi's emissaries know how to envelop themselves in the wind. Hunger, the terrifying companion of the dry season, is held to be a very close relative of the *wanülü* and behaves in the same way. In this he, too, is clearly associated with Pulowi (lines 6025–7007).

On the Side of Life, on the Side of Death

For the Guajiro, Pulowi is essentially the giver of death (*oukta*). She kills directly or else takes people away from life on earth (lines 424–428, 611–636, 915–928, 2033–2046). All *pulowi* places are extremely dangerous and often deadly (lines 518–533, 666–689; pp. 80–81 above). For instance, the *pulowi* stone called Palasapain, located near the shore in the bay of Neimalu in Colombian Guajira, is so dangerous that children who pass near it die at once. The same thing is said of the Pulowi of Mashierü and of most of the *pulowi* places. All the emissaries of Pulowi can bring death. Among them, the *wanülü* is the most active and the most feared. Here is a dramatic account of the way he goes about killing:

> The *wanülüs* whistle.
> They make people tremble.
> They paralyze those who hear their cries.
> The hearts of those who are seen by a *wanülü* beat violently.
> If a *wanülü* has shot arrows at them, they die.
> They feel their bodies tremble,
> they vomit red blood all the way home.
> Their bodies are bathed in sweat.
> The arrow has gone right into them
> and that is why they vomit blood.
> The blood does not flow outside the body but inside it.
> The *wanülü* has made them die . . .

Partly responsible for drought, Pulowi is also, over and above hunger, responsible for death. And, were I not afraid of oversimplifying, she could be said to symbolize the hostility and meanness of the natural environment. Finally, Pulowi is herself pathogenic. She contaminates the places she frequents, which become the sources of mortal diseases (cf. p. 81 above).[48]

Juya is closely associated with life, *kata o'u*. For the Guajiro, rain is synonymous with rebirth or life. Indeed, rain is utterly essential to these horticulturists and stock breeders living in a semidesert region where a year with scant rainfall is a year of death (lines 7008–7079). "Juya is our father, without him we would not be here," say the Guajiro (cf. lines 9001–9003, 10,008). In the myths Juya returns life to Pulowi's victims (lines 433–440). It was on the occasion of the September rains, heralding the main rainy season, that the Guajiro used to organize the "games of the goat," marking by collective agricultural labor the rebirth of community life.

We have seen, however, that the Guajiro also attribute to Juya the power to give death. For they are familiar with the deadly power of lightning, "Juya's weapon," and they have observed the coincidence between the coming of the rains and the occurrence of epidemic diseases that often prove fatal (lines 8087–8095). It was probably to resolve what they felt was a logical difficulty that the Guajiro invented a myth recounting how Juya is led to dispense death in order to free himself from a debt toward the Pulowi clan (lines 8069–8086). According to this tale, Juya killed his brother-in-law, a member of the Pulowi clan, in revenge for his wife's reprehensible behavior. He is then obliged by Guajiro law, if he wants to avoid war, to make compensation to that clan. However, the Pulowi clan, instead of asking him for damages in the form of cattle or jewels as is customary, demands that he provide it with dead Guajiros; for Pulowi is reputed to drink their blood (cf. lines 407–412). In this way the Guajiro show that if Juya kills, it is always Pulowi who bears the responsibility. Thus they render the opposition between Juya and life, on the one hand, and Pulowi and death, on the other, less equivocal.

On the Side of the Animals, on the Side of the Hunter

The misadventures of overskillful hunters or fishermen swallowed up by Pulowi have already been discussed at length. It is often while pursuing a game animal "sent by Pulowi" that they are suddenly devoured; for Pulowi is the "mistress" of game animals and of all the "wild animals of the earth and the water." Deer, brockets, and so on are to her what cattle are to the Guajiro.[49] More than that, she charms and subjugates them; they are at her mercy.[50] She is willing to concede to men a few head from her "flock," but on the condition that they do not overdo it. Finally, all *pulowi* places are characterized by an abundance of wild animals (e.g., lines 666–670, 2063–2067).

Juya is the "master" of hunters. I emphasized this when I referred to his weapons and his "hypermasculinity." He hunts or has others hunt the game animals that abound in his lands (lines 277–318). In this he is "the enemy of Pulowi." Some animals, however, are said to be the "sons of Juya." They are the ones that the Guajiro associate with the rain; they include both *jokoche*,[51] "brown lizard," a kind of small earth-colored *anolis* who is reputed to announce rain by extending "in the direction of the lightning" the large red and yellow membrane he has under his neck, and the dragonfly, *pachanoi*. For the Guajiro, the latter is the very mark of the rain,[52] for scarcely has a shower fallen in one place than swarms of dragonflies appear elsewhere, as though born by spontaneous generation. But, although in the myths these animals commonly serve as the messengers of Juya, they are nonetheless regarded as *she'e ma*, "products of the earth," in the same way as all other wild animals.

Cultivated Plants and Wild Plants

Juya is closely linked to horticulture. In his domain there is a plentiful supply of all the best fruits and cultivated plants: muskmelon, watermelon, maize, beans, and more. "Without him there would be no domestic plants (*attie*)." The fruits of Juya have the property of being "concentrated" food: a very small quantity of them is enough to satisfy one's hunger (lines 272–276). One myth, not included here, tells how in the twinkling of an eye Juya and his nephews sowed the garden (*apain*, or *yüja*) of a Guajiro who, no later than the next day, was able to enjoy the harvest. "Here is Juya, let us prepare our seeds.[53] Here is Juya, the meadows are going to appear, we shall be able to put our cattle out to graze," the Guajiro say in the way of a dictum. As soon as the first rain has fallen, they go off in couples to sow their gardens. A few days later, with exceptional rapidity, the new shoots appear and start growing "because of Juya."[54]

Near *pulowi* places there is always an abundance of fruits or wild plants.[55] It is mainly in such places that the Guajiro find the precious roucou from which they make a dye (*paliisa*) and the maguey whose fibers they use for weaving. There also are found the rare plants used in the composition of *lanias*, priceless amulets that serve many purposes. Some Guajiros go and gather them there, taking a large number of precautions but still exposing themselves to great danger, for such plants are dangerous (lines 671–689). It is not uncommon for people to disappear during such expeditions or to be seriously ill when they come back, which largely accounts for the economic value and immense prestige attached to *lanias*. Finally, the myths sometimes describe the subterranean realm of Pulowi as a place where there is an abundance of berries and fruits of all kinds, the gathering (*atpaja*) of which was frequently organized by the Guajiro during the period when their gardens were not producing.[56]

The Cold and the Hot

In classifications specific to the shamans (which will not be elaborated on here) Juya is sometimes associated with Saamatui, "a cold desert land where nothing is encountered that is capable of harming man"[57] and where only the shaman can go, with his or her *spirit*. Furthermore, with Juya the Guajiro associate *jemiai*, the period of relative cold accompanied by a slight wind that immediately follows the "main rainy season." They frequently oppose it to *jouktai*, the strong, hot, parching wind linked with Pulowi.

Pulowi, on the contrary, is associated by the shamans with the "hot lands," *walachipa'a* (from *walachi*, "heat"). This association is so clear that some of them use the word *poulouliruje* (from *poulouli*; cf. chapter 2, n. 14) to designate those same places, contrasting with *samatulüje*, "the place of the cold."

The Light and the Dark

But there are some shamans who, in their theories regarding sickness, more readily set in opposition a world of light—*waratui, waratüsü*—to which belong all those who are in good health, and a world of darkness—*piyushi, piuushisü*—into which "the souls of the sick Guajiros penetrate."[58] Over this world reign all the beings linked to Pulowi who dispense death. It is there that the *spirits* of the shamans go in order to take away the souls of their patients. But, they assert, it is only in the "world of light" that their *spirits* encounter Juya.

This opposition between light and darkness is manifestly correlative with an opposition between the day—*ja'ipa ka'i*—and the night—*aipa* or *sawai*. The Guajiro consider night to be full of dangers, for Pulowi and her emissaries almost always operate between sunset and sunrise (lines 996–1002, 2089–2094, 5030–5031, 5058–5061).[59] But it is also at night, during dreams, that human souls leave their bodies to wander in that fearful world. And it is at night that one's shadow—*oyolojo* or *ajuya*—vanishes completely, the shadow that, according to the Guajiro, is proof of the presence of the *soul* and hence of individual existence (lines 5–8). This is why, even just before the rainy season when the wind has dropped and the heat has become unbearable,[60] many Guajiros prefer to sleep in the stifling atmosphere of a hermetically sealed house rather than arouse the dangers of the night by opening the door to let the air in.

A Legitimate Couple

Juya and Pulowi are husband and wife. All Pulowis are Juya's wives. The Guajiro unanimously agree on this point and do not fail to emphasize it on every occasion (e.g., lines 401–403, 690–691, 720–722). Further, the union of Juya and Pulowi reproduces the polygynous, matrilocal Guajiro marriage in which the man, unique and mobile, shares his time among his wives, fixed, manifold, and generally scattered over a vast territory.

Thus the Guajiro world closes upon itself. The two mythical beings Juya and Pulowi who assume a number of apparently incompatible fundamental oppositions unite to form a legitimate couple. Seen from this perspective, what was opposition becomes, rather, complementarity. And this complementarity is expressed in a variety of ways. It may take the form of alternation, the successive supremacy of first one, then the other of the "opposing principles." Natural phenomena set the example: alternation of day and night, alternation during the year of rain and drought. It may take the form of an always threatened and precarious coexistence. The Guajiro couple is an illustration of this: although married, the Guajiro man and woman are potential enemies, for they belong to groups whose interests often conflict. And finally, this complementarity may be expressed through a ceaseless fight. Commonly, in the myths, Juya and Pulowi confront one another directly. The fate of humankind depends in theory on the outcome of this combat.

But in this confrontation Juya always triumphs over Pulowi (lines 441–470, 623–638, etc.). "He is the only one who can stand up to her . . . because she is his wife," say the Guajiro.[61] In proclaiming his victory, they display their optimism. For Juya is associated with an essential element, water, necessary for the perpetuation of all life. Juya must conquer the drought—sometimes with human assistance (lines 7049–7079); life must triumph over death. But they also display their belief in male supremacy, since, in their own words, "man must always be above woman . . . on all occasions!"

The rivalry between Juya and Pulowi, however, pales into insignificance when the concern is to teach people certain rules of life. Pulowi encourages hunters and fishermen not to abuse the natural environment. Juya urges marriageable young women not to abuse society by remaining secluded too long.

Care must therefore be taken not to regard Guajiro religion as manichean. Although associated with a number of negative qualities, Pulowi does not embody Evil. For she is also the mistress of game animals: parsimoniously she surrenders to men some animals from her "herd." Similarly, it would be an oversimplification to say that Juya personifies Good.

Through an analysis of "The Journey to the Beyond: A Guajiro Eurydice," we shall now see how the oppositions educed in this chapter come into play and show to what extent they make it possible to "decode" a myth.

3. The Journey to the Beyond

We die three times: the first time in our flesh, the second time in the heart of those who survive us, and the third time in their memory . . . which is our final and chilliest tomb. (J. Green, *Varouna*)

"The Journey to the Beyond" is one of the best-known myths of the Guajiro Indians. For this reason I was able to collect twelve versions of it originating from various parts of the Indian zone. The version reproduced in full in Part One above is the one with the greatest amount of detail. It will serve as reference. Here is a short summary of it to help the reader follow the thread of the analysis:

1. Through his excessive weeping, a Guajiro Indian prompts his dead wife to come back to him on earth.
   She leads him to Jepira, the land of the dead.
2. The Guajiro stays there some time with his wife. Out of patience with the debauched life she leads there, he decides to return home.
3. The Guajiro takes the wrong road. He wanders around for a long time before reaching Juya's domain.
   After he has passed certain tests, Juya invites him to stay.
   Because he does not heed Juya's advice, he is killed by Pulowi.
   Juya resuscitates him and has him brought back to earth.
4. The Guajiro recounts his adventure, despite the recommendations of his "carrier."
   He dies.

Part 3 of this myth will receive the fullest attention because it is the one that, to my mind, contains the most profound and original message. But first it is essential to examine each of the episodes belonging to parts 1 and 2, for in order to grasp their meaning and significance it is necessary to understand their ethnographic background. This systematic study will also show that a myth is not necessarily a homogeneous form of expression, in that each of its different parts may be marked to varying degrees by symbolism and esoterism. "The Journey to the Beyond" affords a very good example of this heterogeneity. Thus, in the third part of the tale, the logic governing the oppositions and metaphorical analogies is fully developed, while in the first two parts, more directly discernible cultural elements come into play. Moreover, this difference is reflected in the way in which the Guajiro relate or receive the myth. The first two parts, which are more anecdotal in form, are known by a large number of storytellers, and the listeners grasp directly what happens in them. Far fewer are those who are familiar with the last two parts. And I witnessed occasions when some listeners, the most practical-minded, were clearly put out at not being able immediately to perceive their meaning.

JEPIRA, THE LAND OF THE DEAD GUAJIRO

The Dead Wife's Visit

An Indian listener is not unduly surprised when listening to the episode telling of the return to earth of the hero's dead wife. For the Guajiro believe that the dead can appear in two ways to the living and communicate with them: through the intermediary of supernatural beings known as *yolujas* or through dreams.

Yolujas are the forms taken by dead Indians on arriving in Jepira. They are a second representation of the soul or, in an Indian expression, "the souls of dead Indians": *sa'in wayu ouktüsü*. The Guajiro maintain that they return to earth where they pay short visits in order to pester the living. Vindictive and captious, they are beings of ill omen. This is why people avoid them or flee when they meet them, usually at dusk or dawn, silent, "walking like drunks whose bones have been removed," "shadows" or "hazy silhouettes."[1] "Guajiros die of fright on seeing them."

But generally there is no direct contact or conversation between the living and *yolujas*. They are regarded as silent figures. And it is through dreams that verbal communication with the dead is commonly established. If I dream of a dead man, if I speak to him, if he speaks to me, this means that my *soul* has met his *soul*, which was wandering about somewhere on earth, usually in the form of a *yoluja*.

Whether through the agency of dreams or of the *yoluja*, this fragile connection between the living and the dead is always fleeting and indirect. To establish it, each version of the myth proposes a different anecdote. Here are two examples:

Near his wife's grave
the Guajiro dug a hole.
He stayed there night and day.
At dawn he looked toward it.
Sometimes he had the impression of seeing her alive . . .
One day, late in the afternoon,
he heard a voice that said:
"*Kalüin! Kalüin!* Beloved! Beloved!"
When the sun had set
he saw his wife step out shaking herself, like a partridge.
Dust fell off her dress

and it was as though smoke was being given off by her body.
"I am here, my wife! Don't leave me!"
cried the Guajiro standing up.
But she did not answer . . .

(Extract from Mülieshi Jayaliyu's version of the tale, December 1969)

Here, it is the *yoluja*-woman who, spied on and pursued by her husband, who has entered into a sort of delirium through keeping vigil, is induced to communicate. Pursued all night long, as in the reference version, she breaks the silence once and for all the following morning by inviting him to follow her.

In the second example the connection is made through the agency of the rheum from a dog's eyes. According to the Guajiro, this body fluid has the property, if they put some on their eyes, of rendering visible to humans such supernatural beings as *yolujas* and *wanülüs*; for, they say, dogs, like mules and donkeys, see them "naturally" (cf. Part One, lines 4090–5000).

The myth suggests that by this means the unhappy husband is able to plunge straight into the world inhabited by his wife:

Each evening, at nightfall,
the Guajiro's dog started barking
then running around restlessly.
It was the *yoluja* who had come to join her husband.
The dog recognized her.
"I wonder what it is the dog can see,"
said the man to himself.
The animal had some rheum in the corner of his eyelids.
The Guajiro removed some and smeared it over his eyes.
He then saw his wife arriving.
"Ah! You came, my little wife!"
he said, embracing her.
She did not look like a *yoluja*
but like a living person
and he was able to kiss her.
"I have come because you weep and because you sleep alone."

(Extract from Sepana Epieyu's version of the tale, September 1969)

The Journey to Jepira

Jepira—"the land of the dead Guajiro," "the land of the *yolujas*," "the dwelling-place of the shades of the dead"—is a desolate hill forming part of a mountain peninsula in the northeast of Columbian Guajira. From Salain ("El Cabo" in Colombian), the last inhabited place before Jepira and the normal way of approach, the "land of the dead" has the appearance of an island situated "in the middle of the sea." It is regarded and described as such by most Indians. Very few of them feel a desire to approach it, even less to visit it, for it is considered to be a gloomy and dangerous place. For this reason its being an island is seldom challenged.

Of the episode relating the crossing of the deep bay that separates the shoreline of the "island" from Jepira, there are almost as many variants as there are storytellers. Two will be quoted here, one rich in details and incidents, the other more austere and careful about logic, which shows that a myth always to some extent reflects the personality of the narrator:

> They set out at dawn.
> When the sun was very hot
> they lay down in the shadow of a tree.
> The man saw his wife's white legs.
> He drew near.
> "Leave me alone!" she said.
> He wanted to couple with her.
> "Since you are my wife, I can sleep with you."
> "No! You must sleep alone,
> or else I won't take you with me."
> They began walking again.
> At nightfall they arrived near Jepira.
> On reaching the seashore
> the woman entered the water.
> She told her husband to follow her.
> The man plunged in.
> "You want me to drown!" he cried.
> But the woman blew in his direction.
> The man's feet were lifted up . . .

> (Extract from a tale told by the shaman Setuma Püshaina, August 1973)

In the following version the two heroes travel by night with the result that the Guajiro finds himself in Jepira without having seen anything:

> "We are going to follow this path,
> we'll go toward the east," said the woman.
> They went off far, very far.
> It was nighttime.
> "We are going to stay here,"
> said the woman next day at dawn.
> They had arrived in Jepira . . .

> (Extract from Manulu Jayaliyu's version, July 1973)

The most fastidious storytellers consider this variant to have a dual advantage. It gets around the awkward episode of the Guajiro walking

on the waves and permits a more logical entry into the myth: it is during the night that one dreams and is likely to meet *yolujas*. In its beginning at least, then, they regard the myth as a dream becoming a reality.

The episode in which Bittern distributes the water is not featured in
all the versions of the myth. But there is a twofold justification for this
bird having the role of water-giver at the entrance to Jepira. For, on the
one hand, the Guajiro relate that bitterns always go off to die in "the
land of the *yolujas*":

> When bitterns feel that their end is near
> they ask their kin to take them to Jepira.
> Over there is the land of their clan.
> Like us, they prefer to die on their lands.

On the other hand, they associate the bittern with water: "Where
there is a bittern, there is water!" "When bittern sings, it is going to
rain!" they say in the way of proverbs. In addition, *karaisüin*, literally
"bitterns' drink," is the name given to the short rains that sometimes
precede the rains of *juyo'u* (Arcturus).

It is therefore not surprising to find Jokoche, "Brown Lizard," in the
place of Bittern in a variant of that episode:

> They came to Brown Lizard's abode.
> "There you are, grandson," he said to the man.
> In the eyes of the Guajiro, Brown Lizard had human form.
> He sent for a small gourd
> that the woman might drink.
> She drank ten small gourds full.
> "What about you?" Brown Lizard asked the Guajiro.
> "I am thirsty, grandfather!" the man replied.
> Brown Lizard sent for a small gourd
> that his grandson might drink.
>
> (Extract from a tale told by Ramansita Uliyu, July 1973)

For Brown Lizard is Juya's son and *shira jokoche*, literally "lizard's
piss," designates the very fine rain that others call *karaisüin*, "bitterns'
drink."

Finally, the presence of a door at the entrance to Jepira suggests that
the world of the dead is invisible to humans. No hope, then, of the
living seeing the *yolujas* on the "island" of Jepira: "they are behind the
stone which is like a door." For some Guajiros, this door is the place
where living beings are transformed into *yolujas*. It is there that the *soul*
assumes its new form, "there where the *yolujas* come to the newly
dead."[2]

1. Iisho Jayaliyu practicing on the drum (*kaashi*) before the beginning of a *yonna* dance. Pararu, September 1975.

2. Guajiro living area: the house (*miichi*) where the hammocks are hung up at night, the sunroof (*luma*), and, in the background at far left, the "kitchen" (*kusinaþia*), demarcated by a fence made of branches. The roof of the house is in *yotojolo*, i.e., it is made of the woody strands that the Guajiro remove from the heart of the *yosu* torch cacti. Wüinkua, January 1970.

3. A traditional kitchen enclosed by cut torch cacti half-buried in the ground (which keeps them alive). On the left, leaning against the fence, a "fig-gatherer" (*lumia*). Koushotki (Jalaala sierra, Colombia), August 1973.

4. Provisional shelter occupied by a family fleeing the drought. The fence made of planks (on the left) provides protection against the east wind. On the right, the "kitchen." Alitajain (northeast of Pararu), August 1969 (from slide).

5. Landscape in southern Guajira: torch cactus (*kayuusi*); house with adobe walls and *yotojolo* roof. Between Maicao and Paraguaipoa, February 1970.

6. "Antoonia Kocheera" Jayaliyu, a Guajiro hunter. The bow (*uraichi*) and arrows (*jatü*) are hardly used anymore nowadays. The loincloth (*aiche,* or *wusi*), the belt (*si'ira*) with pompoms, and the shirt (*kamiisa*) constitute the traditional dress of the Guajiro man of modest means. The hat (*woma*), made by the Guajiro, is definitely of Western inspiration. Chuaralu (north of Wüinkua), December 1969.

7. The search for water: sinking a well in the bed of a "rio" at the approach of the dry season. Kojua, December 1968 (from slide).

8. Iilia Jayaliyu, daughter of Iisho Jayaliyu, her face covered with *mashuka,* a black powder made from the spores of mushrooms and commonly used "as protection against the heat of the sun." Wüinkua, July 1975.

9. Rajiina Jitnu, "an old woman who knows a great deal." Kasusain, November 1969.

10. Makaerü Jitnu weaving the attachments (*enna*) of a hammock. Pararu, September 1969.

11. Mariia Apüshana polishing an earthenware jar (*jula'a*) with the help of a rounded stone. Mariia is a potter at Iramasira (north of Kusi). August 1975.

12. Scene from a "first burial," near the cemetery, a few hours before the coffin is put in the grave. The women weep around the coffin, their faces covered. The men drink. Waraima (north of Pararu), July 1975.

13. Women weeping during the funeral wake. The sheet wound around the coffin perhaps takes the place of the cowskin that used to be wrapped around the corpse, unless this is merely a custom borrowed from the West. Maüya (northwest of Wüinkua), July 1973.

14. Equidae skulls fixed on a fence "to keep away the *yolujas.*" Palawajain (in Colombia, north of Wüinkua), August 1975.

15. An ancient cemetery uncovered by the wind. In the shattered urns can be seen the remains "put in order" at the time of the second burial. Here, most of them have been placed in individual urns (*wushu*). Mojuai (east of Wüinkua), August 1973.

16. Woman and child returning from the market. The marks on the woman's face are the remains of face paint. The little girl is wearing a "good health" necklace. Aulejemerai, September 1969 (from slide).

17. "Koroliina" Jitnu, daughter of Iisho Jayaliyu and Makaerü Jitnu, aged about ten. Ayajui, September 1975.

18. The *yonna* dance. The man, wearing the *karatsü,* has his face painted with roucou (*pali'isa*); the motif is called *juyasa'aya* (Juya's legs). The woman is covered in the *pannerü ko'usü.* The motif of the roucou painting that covers her face is known as *jerüi'chepuya.* Pararu, October 1973.

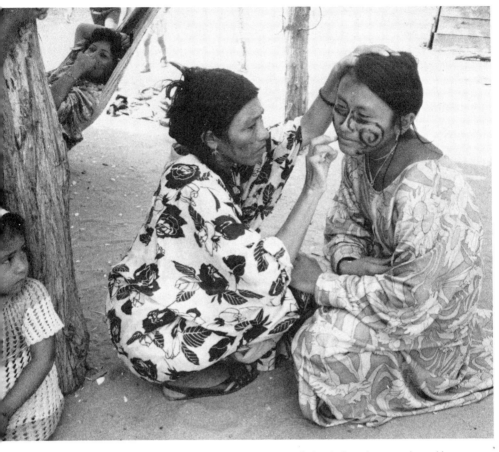

19. Application of a linear design in roucou on a girl's face before the *yonna* dance. Here it is the motif known as *sawainrü'chepuya* (painting of the marine turtle). Pararu, October 1973.

20. Couple going to market to sell goats. Kousharaichon (near Pararu), October 1969.

21. Returning from market. Neima, December 1969.

22. Market scene. Piruachon (Los Filuos), near Paraguaipoa, July 1969.

23. A family on the point of emigrating. Koushotki, Jalaala sierra, Colombia, August 1973.

24. A new game . . . Pararu, September 1973.

The Stay in Jepira

According to Guajiro descriptions a society exists in Jepira that from the point of view of the economy, the political system, and social organization reproduces the society of the living. There the rich—those who own large herds—remain rich. There they find again all the livestock slaughtered by their kinfolk during the funeral wake that preceded their burial (lines 140–141). Similarly, in Jepira the kinship relations that are largely the basis of Guajiro political power remain unchanged.

But so far as food and sexual or marital morals are concerned, Jepira is the opposite of the terrestrial world. It is this reversal that many storytellers take pains to describe with the greatest insistence. In Jepira the hero finds an abundance of rich and varied food that does not even need to be cooked, whereas in the Indian territory food is scarce, is difficult to obtain, and requires lengthy preparation. In Jepira the wife refuses to couple with her husband, whereas in real life the Guajiro are quick to point out women's sexual duties toward their husbands. What is more, in the world of the dead the wife has "several husbands,"[3] whereas the Guajiro laud the virtues of polygyny, do not recognize polyandry, and severely condemn adultery on the part of women[4] while being very indulgent toward male adultery. Finally, in Jepira the heroine is mobile and enterprising. She constantly moves from one place to another and takes initiatives that should be the preserve of men. She decides by herself to go dancing or alone takes an active part in the sexual act. Her husband, however, is compelled to remain immobile, to await her, and to observe. Now, the Guajiro man is essentially mobile, as has already been stressed. He lives outside (*anoitpa*) a great deal, busy tending his herds, hunting, or fishing. Polygynous, he has to go from one wife to another. The Guajiro woman travels more rarely and within a far smaller area. She is socially "fixed" throughout nearly all her life and remains theoretically united to her matrilineage, living quite close to her mother's place after her marriage.

It is no doubt to psychoanalysis that we should look for greater insight into the meaning of this inversion of behavior patterns in the world of the dead. It might be able to interpret the fantasies of a society that obliges some of its men to be polygynous and to become perpetual wanderers and condemns its women to immobility and to long periods of sexual privation. This point will not be developed here, but it is worth noting that this sexual aspect is central to some versions of the myth. Here is an example:

> The wife did not want her husband to take her . . .
> Near the dance floor girls were lying,
> their legs apart.

"What would happen if I coupled with one of them?"
the Guajiro wondered.

He lay with one girl
but he did not have any feeling of sexual embrace.
Everything was different.
The woman did not seem to have any flesh.
She was like a liquid, without resistance.[5]

The following night,
because he had coupled with a *yoluja*,
the Guajiro changed form.
Up to then he had known where he was from.
Now he had forgotten everything.

He could no longer find the way to the earth.
He had become a *yoluja*.

(Extract from a tale told by Mülieshi Jayaliyu, December 1969)

In two versions of the myth the copulation of the hero with his dead wife or with other *yoluja*-women has the effect of making him pass immediately from the world of the dead to the world of Juya. In other variants, however, this sexual act is penalized by the return of the hero to earth, chased by angry *yolujas* or brought back by various "carriers."[6] In these truncated versions the Guajiro generally lay greater emphasis on those aspects that point up what they all consider to be the moral of this myth, namely, that it is futile, dangerous, or ridiculous to want to "live with the dead" by losing oneself entirely in one's memories. Over there in Jepira they live happily without a thought for the living! It is necessary to start life all over again. It is necessary to take another wife. You should concern yourself with the dead only because they oblige you to. Otherwise "they come back to earth in the form of *yolujas* to threaten you and plague you all the time . . ."

Moreover, there are several other myths in which a similar rule of conduct vis-à-vis the dead is indirectly recommended. Here is an example:

Two brothers loved each other dearly.
The elder died.
He was buried beneath a tree, near his house,
as was the custom in former times.

Each day the younger visited him.
He wept by his tomb.
Such had long been his wont
when he encountered an *alijuna*.
"Why do you weep?" he asked.
The *alijuna* was alive, like the Guajiro.

He was not a *yoluja.*
"I am weeping for my dead brother."
"Do you want to see him?"
"I would love to see him again!"
"I'll take you there, to Jepira, the abode of the *yolujas.*"

The *alijuna* would sell alcohol there to the *yolujas.*[7]
They would get drunk.
That was his business.
The *alijuna* was alive,
but the *yolujas* did him no harm.

At nightfall
the *alijuna* told the Guajiro to get ready.
It took them three days to reach Jepira.
There the *alijuna* hid the Guajiro.
He put him under a barrel with a small hole in it.
The Guajiro saw his brother
drunk among the drunken *yolujas.*

"What a fragrance! What is it that smells of muskmelon?[8]
Give it to us, *alijuna!*" the *yolujas* said.
For them the living Guajiro smelled of muskmelon.
The dead brother went up to the *alijuna.*
"Go away! Go back with my brother
or else I'll hand him over to the *yolujas!*
I don't want to see him!"
The *yoluja* threatened the *alijuna.*

And so he had to leave without being paid.
They took three days to get back.
"Your brother did not want to see you."
The *alijuna* repeated to the Guajiro his brother's words.
"He drove me away and yet we loved one another!"

On his return, the Guajiro disinterred his brother.
He went and got some wood and burned his bones.
Then he buried the ashes.
Thus he caused him to die forever.

The *alijuna* returned among the *yolujas:*
"Have you seen the *yoluja* who spoke to you last time?"
they asked him.
"He has vanished," they added;
"We haven't seen him for several days."

The *alijuna* went and told the Guajiro:
"Your brother's no longer in Jepira."

"Good! So he's dead, then, he has disappeared!"
he said.

The Guajiro was light of heart.
The *yoluja* was dead for his bones had been burnt.
(Recounted by Sepana Epieyu on September 8, 1969.)

Here, finally, is another tale that attests to the unfaithfulness of the dead; it is regarded by the Guajiro who recount it as a "true-life story":

There was a Guajiro whose wife was dead.
He loved her dearly.
He wept for her continually.
Every night he went to where she was buried
and he started to weep.

One night he met her.
She was singing.
She was a *yoluja*.
This is what she sang:
"Why has this man come here to weep?
I'm waiting for my beloved Jisenta, he's on his way to me!"
Jisenta was her father's dead brother.

"Look how this woman is behaving!
She sings! She's with another man!
And I who weep continually!
Why should I weep?"

The Guajiro went and set fire to the sunroof,
the sunroof beneath which his wife was buried.
Immediately afterward he left.

The woman's kinfolk saw the flames and the smoke.
"Who set that alight?" they asked in anger.
They followed the Guajiro's tracks.
They wanted to kill him.

But it was he who killed them all.
Other members of his wife's family went after him.
He killed them as well. . . ."[9]

(Recounted by Rosa Epieyu on September 7, 1969. About thirty-five years old, Rosa lives at Kousharaichon, in Venezuelan Guajira.)

THE REALM-BEYOND-DEATH

Adopting a synthetic approach, I shall show that the third part of the myth partly reflects Guajiro conceptions of a realm beyond death and of a cycle ensuring the perpetuation of life and hence of society.

What is striking in the descriptions of this world that lies beyond Jepira where the action now unfolds is the simultaneous presence of Juya and Pulowi and, indeed, the fact that they are the main protagonists. What, then, is the significance of the dual presence of these two beings whose importance was emphasized earlier?

After his stay in Jepira, the world of the *yolujas*, our hero goes to the abode of Juya and Pulowi. He is then brought back to earth, where he stays for a short time before returning to Jepira. This cyclic development of the myth raises questions as to what the Guajiro say about the fate of their dead.

We have just seen that a *yoluja* can die. "All people die twice; once here, once in Jepira. Then they get lost":[10] so it is frequently said. What becomes of them then? Questioned on this, no Guajiro can answer; but many of them indirectly provide the beginnings of an answer.

The Rains and the Dead

The Guajiro establish indisputable links between the rain and the dead. Such a link is explicit in the myth entitled "Juya's Debt":

> The rains are abundant because Juya got into trouble.
> Now, to pay for this death,
> he has to gather people and animals.
> Men give their dead to Juya.
> In exchange, Juya gives rain to the families of the dead. (cf. lines 8069–8086)

Similarly, the elders frequently relate the following anecdote:

> When they heard the thunder of Juya,
> when they heard the thunder of Iiwa,
> the Guajiro-beside-the-sea, the *parauja*, began to weep
> for then they recalled their dead kin.
> But at the same time they said:
> "The rain brings food,
> and soon we'll be able to eat our fill."

For some Guajiros, the rains unquestionably "come from the dead":

> Juya—the Rain—is nothing other than the long-dead Guajiro.
> Moreover, when it is going to rain, one dreams of the dead.
> The elders have learned this from experience. (cf. lines 8096–9000)

There are even some who state that "when the rain falls, it always comes from the direction of Jepira."[11] Others recount stories that they consider to have "actually happened" to demonstrate the existence of close links between the rains and the dead. Here is an example:

One night my maternal uncle was visited by a brother of his,
a brother who had long been dead.
He was a *yoluja*.
"I have come to collect[12] some money,
for I am a prisoner.[13]
To set me free they're asking a great deal!" he said.
My uncle was in his house with members of his family.
The *yoluja* was outside, beneath the sunroof.
They had all heard him speaking.
"I'll come back tomorrow to get what you can give me.
I'm off now to see another brother,"
the *yoluja* said.
My uncle went and sold some cattle to get some money.
"Who can be keeping him prisoner?
Can it be Juya?" he wondered.
Beneath the sunroof he set out some food
along with the money demanded.
In the evening the *yoluja* returned.
"That's just what I wanted, there's nothing missing!
Now I'll be off.
I'll come back soon."

My uncle thought that he wouldn't eat,
that he would leave the money.
"He's no longer a person, he can't take the money with him!
He'll just take its *soul*," he said to himself.
But the next day he found nothing left,
neither money, nor food.
"Why has my brother done this?"
my uncle wondered.

The following day
heavy rain fell on my uncle's house.
Much water flowed through his garden.
He had a very plentiful harvest.

His brother had been dead for years.
After that he never came back.

(Recounted by Mapua Uraliyu, alias Eugenio Fernández, on October 19,
1969.)

These anecdotes, which provide irrefutable proof of the fact that the
fate of the dead is linked to the rains, sometimes serve also to justify
flagrant meteorological injustices:

One of their kinfolk came back to earth
in the form of rain.

He made a gift of much water to his sons and nephews.
Thus they became rich.
Their uncle had taken pity on them.
He fell as rain upon their lands.
Juyakaka nia:
He had become rain.

But generally, the dead who "turn into rain" remain anonymous:

Those who make the rain are nameless.
They are the rain.
"I am he who rains!"
"I am the rain, my grandson!" one hears in dreams.
"Don't be frightened, I am the rain,
and this rain is so you can eat."
But he who dreams cannot recognize the grandfather
or the ancestor who has come to speak to him.

The Wanülüs and the Dead

In the same way, the Guajiro assert that "the *wanülüs* are people who have long been dead."

Some of them, very few it is true, even say explicitly that the *yolujas* become *wanülüs:*

When they are very *yoluja*,
they become *wanülüs*.
Long after death,
not immediately.[14]

Others, less definite, simply say that

the *yoluja* is first a *yoluja*,
then he is a *wanülü*.
He is the *alijuna* the Guajiro meets.[15]
He is the one who goes on foot or on a mount.
He is the *wanülü* who shoots arrows at us and kills us.

Similarly, the myth entitled "Pulowi and the Deerhunter" (lines 940–2067) relates the story of a man who, long after disappearing from the earth, appears before the living in the form of a *wanülü:*

The Guajiro disappeared again.
He had gone back under the earth
like the first time.

It is said that he sometimes comes out
in the form of a completely white deer.
He can take on human appearance.

He transpierces dogs.
He threatens men.

He has become a *wanülü*.

Many variants of this tale are known, most of which have the same ending.

Finally, the shamans assert that their *spirits*—called *asheyus, ajunas,* but also *wanülüs*—are the "*souls* of people who have long been dead," or, much more vaguely, that "they come from Jepira." *

The Guajiro thus identify those who have long been dead either with Juya, since they can turn into rain, or with Pulowi, since they can turn into *wanülüs*. This is the essential message of the third part of "The Journey to the Beyond." In it, the Guajiro hero experiences this dual presence of Juya and Pulowi in a realm-beyond-death that leads directly to life on earth and invests it with its fundamental character. For this life on earth is marked by the simultaneous presence of "principles" associated with life and "principles" associated with death. This is what is asserted here by the Guajiro, since for them, as will be recalled, symbolically and really the rains are the guarantors of life and the *wanülüs* the bringers of death.

It is by playing with the homological relation

rains : wanülüs :: Juya : Pulowi**

which follows from the analyses in chapter 2 that the myth expresses this message metaphorically.

According to the Guajiro, then, humans are caught up in a fatal cycle. It leads them first from life to death, from life on earth to Jepira, from the state of the "individual"—*wayu*—to the state of *yoluja*. They then find themselves in a nameless, placeless realm-beyond-death where they are assimilated either by Juya or by Pulowi. Finally, associated with the rains or the *wanülüs*, they return to earth (Fig. 1).

This cycle gives meaning to death: life on earth is marked by the presence of the dead and the dead are necessary to it. What is more, it testifies to a human presence even in areas that are the province of nature: climatic phenomena, diseases and death, and, indirectly, fauna and flora.

---

* The reasons for, and consequences of, this paradoxical denomination of the shaman's spirits will be thoroughly studied in a forthcoming book on Guajiro shamanism.

** This convenient formulation was introduced by Lévi-Strauss (1964). The sign : signifies "is to"; the sign ::, expressing a homological relation, signifies "what." The formula therefore reads: the rains are to the *wanülüs* what Juya is to Pulowi.

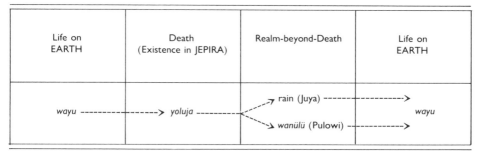

Figure I

By this means the Guajiro have rejected—or at least pushed back—the idea of nature—as though, implicitly, they wanted, through a highly anthropocentric view of the world, to make themselves believe that humankind is ultimately in the essence of beings and things.[16]

Starting from the myth called "The Journey to the Beyond," I have sought to bring out in its entirety the Guajiro conception of death, although this tale alone provides a very incomplete image of it. To achieve this result, it was also necessary to draw on various Indian commentaries and the findings of a prior analysis covering a huge body of oral literature. In fact I did not meet a single Indian who had a clear-cut awareness of the cycle referred to. Although the Guajiro commonly claim that "the dead go to Jepira" or that "the rains and the *wanülüs* are Indians who have long been dead," they very seldom speak of the transition from the state of *yoluja* to that of rain or of *wanülü*, and even less do they allude to the circumstances surrounding such a transition. Patently, the great majority of them do not entertain this problem explicitly. For some Guajiros, however, those who have died through being struck by lightning will undoubtedly become rain later, while "those who have been pierced by the arrows of a *wanülü* will themselves become *wanülüs*, together with those who have been poisoned."[17] Furthermore, the story "Pulowi and the Deerhunter" reveals to us that a man abducted by Pulowi can reappear much later in the form of a *wanülü*. This is as far as any attempt at division usually goes.[18]

Is there not another way in which the Guajiro reveal that the destiny of the dead does not come to an end in Jepira? Indeed there is: their funeral rites reflect their conception of the beyond.

GUAJIRO BURIAL

"A Guajiro is dead!" The shaman has withdrawn, powerless to do any more. The dead man's close kin cover his corpse and leave him alone for awhile. Thus his *soul* can prepare to leave familiar places and people. Soon after, his body is washed by kinswomen, dried, dressed in his finest clothes, and adorned with jewels or prized objects. Wrapped up in a large piece of cloth, it is then placed temporarily in a hammock. Then with the ritual weeping, *ayalaja*, begins the funeral wake proper, known as *alapaja*. It is marked by a large gathering of men and women who, notified by messengers, may come from areas far away from the place of the ceremony. These are kinfolk belonging to the same clan, kinfolk by alliance, neighbors or friends whose number depends essentially on the status of the deceased. With time the throng becomes denser (Photograph 12). The women take turns in weeping (Photograph 13). The men, often drunk with alcohol, engage in increasingly noisy conversations. Everyone takes advantage of this unforeseen opportunity for meeting to tackle the most varied subjects.

One or two days after the death the body is wrapped in cowhide or laid out in a coffin, in accordance with a practice inherited from the West.[19] When the appointed time for the burial, *ojoita*, draws near—three or four days or even a month after the death, so it is said, according to the status of the deceased—the coffin is carried from the place where it is exhibited to where it will be put into the earth.[20] It is again exhibited beneath a sunroof near the future burial place (*ojoitüi* or *ojoijüi*). There the wake can go on for several days more. Amid increased wailings the body is at last lowered into the vault or grave, which is closed or filled in by the kinsmen who opened or dug it out.[21] Provisions that "will serve during the journey to Jepira" are often placed beside the coffin beforehand. There the dead person will find the animals sacrificed during the funeral ceremony. In an atmosphere increasingly marked by alcohol and fatigue, the wake may go on for yet another few days. It is at this stage that the men challenge one another to shooting contests using blanks (*ashanajirawa*) and that long-standing rivalries can degenerate into cruel combats.

Those who have been in contact with the deceased's body during this ceremony do not have to undergo any particular rite other than that of carefully washing their hands and bathing.[22] But after this first burial it is forbidden to pronounce the dead person's name, and it would be dangerous to do so.[23] Anyone who violates this rule is obliged in theory to make a compensatory payment to the deceased person's next-of-kin. Nor should any newborn babies be given the name of someone who has recently died.

A few years after this first burial—generally three years later at least—the dead person's skeleton is dug up and then becomes the focal point of a further ceremony, called "the ordering," *anajawa*, or more precisely "the ordering of the bones," *anajawat jipü*. Like the previous one, it is marked by ritual weeping, a large gathering, and the con-

sumption of food and drink, but on a smaller scale. The prior extraction and arrangement of remains are said to be effected very discreetly.[24]
A man opens the tomb and removes the corpse from the coffin or cowskin in which it is wrapped. A close kinswoman of the dead person, usually belonging to that person's lineage, her head and body partly enve-
loped in a large piece of cloth, her hands wrapped in a handkerchief or
wearing gloves, sorts and cleans the bones. She places them in a terra-
cotta urn, the *pacheshi*, in a close-meshed net bag, or, nowadays, in a
cloth bag, held by another woman. Very often, several corpses belonging to the same matrilineage are removed at the same time from the
various places where they were buried. Then all the receptacles con-
taining the bones are exhibited for the duration of the wake at the home
of the deceased's kinfolk or beneath a sunroof set up near the cemetery
reserved for the remains.[25] These will then be transferred to the unique
huge urn (*pachisha*) in which the remains of all the dead of the matriclan or matrilineage are heaped. Nowadays they are often deposited
in a small vault made of cement.[26]

After this second burial no further attention is given to the remains.
Amuloiresü: "They are lost forever," say the Guajiro. No further ceremony or commemoration is devoted to the dead.

But, contrary to what happens on the occasion of the first burial, the
contacts that the women responsible for preparing the second burial
have with the mortuary remains are considered to be fraught with consequences—not only for them but also for all those who enter into relation, even indirectly, with them. For such women are said to transmit
the disease that shamans call *apülainwa jipü,* "contagion through bones"
(cf. Chapter 2, note 18). It is alleged that after performing this task
they contaminate all they touch, living beings and inanimate objects
alike. Consequently, in order to mitigate this danger, they have to take
as little food as possible for a few days following their intercession and
to receive it exclusively from the hands of others. Some people even
claim that "to do things properly indeed, they should absolutely not use
their hands."

To two successive realms of the beyond there correspond, then, two
burials. But this analogy is not one of pure form. For the Guajiro, the
yolujas are the recent dead, they are known, they have an "identity."
They can be recognized, they can be identified when they come and
haunt the living in their dreams or return to earth. To guard against this
ominous return, care must be taken not to name them. Likewise, the
corpse of one who has recently died retains its identity until the eve of
the second burial.

After their departure from Jepira for a realm-beyond-death, the *yolujas,* having turned into *wanülüs* or rains, become, on the contrary,
anonymous. Similarly, during the second burial the remains of the

dead, mixed up with the old bones, lose all individuality:

corpse : remains :: *yoluja* : *wanülü*
(1st burial) (2nd burial)

This last homological relation perhaps accounts for the far greater virulence that the Guajiro attribute to old bones. Just as a *wanülü* is far more to be feared than a *yoluja*, the corpse at the time of the second burial—on the verge of its second "transformation" and likely to be in league with *wanülüs*—would be far more dangerous to manipulate than it is just after death.[27]

But the ritual, in addition to this basic meaning, has another significance that is perhaps perceived more clearly by the Guajiro: to join to the remains of the anonymous ancestors of the matriclan or matrilineage the remains of one who has died more recently is symbolically to intimate the transition from individual identity to collective identity and also, through this constant accretion, to nurture the hope that the group will last eternally.

THE SOJOURN IN JUYA'S DOMAIN

When considered in detail, the third part of the myth may seem very disconcerting. But the analysis undertaken in the previous chapter reveals its meaning by showing each of its episodes to consist mostly of illustrations of the system of oppositions synthesized by the two mythical beings Juya and Pulowi.

I have made use of some of these episodes to highlight the logical structure of the Guajiro mythical universe and I am fully aware of the tautological character of some of the interpretations that follow. But it is worthwhile to set them out again in another form in this systematic study that, designed as a demonstration, could not but seek to be exhaustive.

The Journey to Juya's Domain

(To get to Juya's domain, the hero of "The Journey to the Beyond" clutches hold of a cow's tail; lines 258–259.)

Like all domestic animals, the cow, which serves here as carrier, guide, and means of locomotion, occupies an ambivalent position in Guajiro thought. As we shall be discussing this point in detail later on, let us just say now, simplifying somewhat, that the Guajiro associate the cow as an animal with Pulowi, while as a domestic animal and a grass-eater they associate it with Juya. The quality of the pastures and the future of the herd depend on the rain, and as Juya is so to speak master of the pastures, it is natural that he should possess large herds. There is, then, nothing surprising in the hero being guided by a cow, since the cow is a symbol of rain and abundance as well as being a "cultivated product."

But in other versions of the myth the carriers are no longer cows but birds whose specific names are not always stated. In the following variant the bird is Nai, the sparrow hawk:

> Junuunai—Black Fly—had seen the Guajiro,
> and he had heard what the *yolujas* had said.
> He went and reported it to Juya.
> "They want to remove that man's bones!" [28]
> Then Juya called Sparrow Hawk.
> "Come here! Go and get that man for me!"

> Black Fly's mount was no good
> and, to bring the man back,
> Juya had preferred to send Sparrow Hawk.
> Sparrow Hawk arrived just as the *yolujas* were advancing,
> one behind the other,
> in order to remove the man's bones.
> "Climb up behind," he said . . .

> . . . The man climbed up behind Sparrow Hawk,
> who brought him beneath the sunroof
> as Juya had commanded.

> (Extract from Ramansita Uliyu's version of the tale, July 1973)

In another variant the carrier is Samulu, the urubu:

> But in Jepira the woman had many husbands.
> The *yolujas* were coupling with her under the Guajiro's eyes,
> her true husband . . .
> . . . An urubu then came toward him
> and took him off on the road that leads to Juya's domain.

These versions that use birds as carriers make a point of situating Juya's world: it is on high, in places that only birds and insects can reach. What is more, when the birds are specified the ones chosen are those reputed to be strong and hardy and therefore able to attain the highest places, furthest from the earth. The urubu, the sparrow hawk, and the "royal vulture," who appear respectively in three versions of this episode, may be so described: a highly popular myth among the Guajiro tells of a competition between them in which what is at stake is the Sun's hat. [29]

The Ordeal of the Boa-Seat

(Juya compels the hero to sit down on a bench that has the appearance of a boa; lines 265–271.)

We have seen (in Chapter 2 above) that in some contexts reptiles are the true metaphorical equivalents of Pulowi. Here, in the domain of Juya, considered to be the traditional enemy of snakes (see lines 8042–8046), the ordeal of the boa-seat thus suggests the presence of Pulowi.

This bench may also be seen as a symbol of immobility, characteristic of Pulowi but, above all, by virtue of the fact that Juya submits snakes to his authority, a sign of his domination over Pulowi, which the Guajiro always seem eager to confirm whenever the occasion presents itself.[30]

Juya's Watermelon

(A single slice was enough to fill the hero up; lines 272–276.)

Juya, as a true "master of horticulture," cannot but possess outstanding fruits or plants. In another version of the myth Juya's watermelons are said to have even more extraordinary properties: "The watermelon formed again as the Guajiro ate it."

The Ordeals of Hunting

(The game and plants that the hero is supposed to bring back to Juya assume human appearance; lines 277–386.)

If we consider, through the six versions of the myth developing this episode, the various ordeals to which the Guajiro is subjected, we can distinguish two major themes. First, Juya asks the man to hunt game animals that in his eyes take on human appearance until he shoots them; they then become game animals again:

I want to eat venison! . . .
The Guajiro met a rich Indian.
He was wearing a red belt, a robe, and a hat. . . .
The Guajiro went off again and shot at the Indian.

(lines 298, 300–301, 310)

Juya then sends him off to gather fruits or cultivated plants which will appear to him in that form only after he has mutilated them:

"I want to eat some gourd!"
"Go and get some!"
The Guajiro met some people with fat bellies, with huge bellies.

(lines 346–348)

Several interpretations can be given for these episodes. The one I shall start with explains particularly well the first theme. It is clear that, in subjecting him to these ordeals, the "hypermasculine" Juya is asking the man to demonstrate his virile qualities in the context of the hunt and war: here the two activities merge into one since the game that Juya asks him to kill in fact assumes human appearance.

But we also know that a *wanülü* sometimes reveals himself in the guise of a man whom one has to kill if one is to survive, and that his corpse always assumes animal form (lines 3004–3011, 5006–5017, 5083–6015). And we have also seen that Pulowi is capable of assuming the appearance of a game animal in order to deceive men. Juya, then, while developing the hero's virile qualities, would appear to be teaching him to beware of appearances and to protect himself against the *wanülü* and Pulowi, who are also his enemies.

A second interpretation reveals a far more profound meaning attaching to this episode. There is a striking analogy between the transformation of men into game or cultivated plants and the transformation mentioned earlier of the long dead into *wanülüs* or rains:

$$\begin{array}{ccc}
 & \text{rains} & \text{cultivated plants} \\
\text{long-dead men :} & :: \text{``virtual'' men :} & \\
 & \textit{wanülüs} & \text{game}
\end{array}$$

But this analogy is strengthened by another relation: the *wanülüs* and Pulowi are the masters of game animals and distribute them to men parsimoniously, while the rains cause cultivated plants to spring up and grow. The *wanülüs* are to the game animals what the rains are to cultivated plants (*wanülüs* : game :: rains : cultivated plants).

It would appear then that this episode, while reflecting fundamental oppositions, makes explicit the idea of the underlying presence of human beings in game animals and cultivated plants by assigning human appearance to them in the realm-beyond-death. It would be, in short, an illustration of that anthropocentric view of the world mentioned earlier. We see how subtle this idea is and how far removed from a belief in reincarnation as animals that some overhasty observers have attributed to the Guajiro.

It should be noted, finally, that in two versions of the myth out of the six that develop this episode there appears a third type of ordeal: Juya commands the hero to go and hunt game that in his eyes takes on the appearance of wild plants:

"I want to eat rabbit. Go and get me some!"
he then said.
He gave the man barbed arrows.
The man saw only dwarf cacti, a great number of them.
He came back when he was tired.

"Well?" asked Juya.
"There's nothing!"
"What did you see?"
"Dwarf cacti."
"That's it!

But shoot your arrow beside them
so as not to destroy the food I collect!"

None of the interpretations suggested above explains this third theme. In fact, another logic governs the correspondences established: the men who turn into animals or plants have, in every case, physical or sartorial characteristics or particular attitudes that justify the choice of the animal or plant in question. According to the version, Indians with large bellies (lines 345–365), generously proportioned women, or *alijunas*—compared with the Guajiro, mestizos or whites are nearly always fat!—represent *kaliiyu* gourds, large and rounded fruits. Men wearing the *karatsü* headdress—a woven crown surmounted by a tuft of large feathers—may, depending on the storyteller, stand for deer, with their tines, or ears of maize with long beards attached to them. A *kusina* Indian wearing a crown made of cassia bark (lines 282–286) represents the brocket, an animal living in remote mountainous areas like ·the *kusina* Guajiro and feeding on large amounts of cassia bark (*aitpa*). A rich man, at the highest point of the Guajiro social hierarchy, suggests the *irama* deer, the preeminently "rich" game animal, the one most sought after and most appreciated by the Guajiro. At this level each storyteller enjoys some degree of freedom in the choice of correspondences. Relating to me "The Journey to the Beyond" at an interval of four years, the same storyteller established different correspondences. The first time, young men wearing a *karatsü* headdress turned into partridges, the second time into deer.

It is clear that all narrators take great pleasure in developing this episode, which enables them, within certain limits, to give evidence of their verve and imagination. Carried away by their own momentum, some did not hesitate to broaden the scope of such correspondences by adding to the two basic themes a third theme exclusively centered on the visual aspect, remaining within the limits of humorous observation and caricature. Thus, to the metamorphoses of human beings into animals or into plants were added metamorphoses of plants into animals. A nopal cactus—*jamüche* or *walaayu*—will be transformed into a rabbit because it sometimes brings forcefully to mind that long-eared animal, or the *jurula* plant laden with fruits that are vaguely suggestive of birds will become a flock of partridges. In such cases it is obvious that only the superficial level of the correspondence has been brought into play, at the expense of the deeper meaning revealed by the analysis, which in this last theme has completely vanished.

The Hero's Death, Resurrection, and Return to Earth

(Pulowi "explodes" and kills the hero. Juya brings him back to life. Spider carries him back to earth; lines 419–479.)

The episode of the Guajiro's death and resurrection serves in a particularly striking way to situate Juya and Pulowi on the side of life and
of death, respectively. But the fact that Pulowi is depicted as a canni-
bal in the reference version has an essentially metaphorical purpose:
Pulowi makes people disappear; she kills them by swallowing them, by
engulfing them (cf. lines 612–636, 2033–2037).

In most of the versions of the myth the return to earth is considered
to be the immediate consequence of the man's disobedience: as soon as
he has brought him back to life, "Juya leads him to Spider so that she
can take him back home."

The most popular carrier is Spider. In another version of the myth,
however, this role is given to Calabash:

Over there lived Calabash, Juya's cook.
"I'll take you to your home
for I was the first to eat my fill with what you collected.
Today I remember.
When they come looking for you I'll keep my head inclined
without uttering a word.
Climb into me!" Calabash ordered.
She started to climb down
and she carried the Guajiro right up to his house
on the west side.

(Extract from Ramansita Uliyu's version of the tale, July 1973)

An inescapable reason for the choice of these surprising intermediaries emerges when one considers that the spider and its thread are
more than a poetic image and more than a means of transport permit-
ting one to travel downward; they are a true symbolic equivalent of the
rain. For, as indicated earlier, Juya is, like all the rains, associated with
a star—*juyo'u*, "the hole of the rain"—through which, according to
some informants, passes the liquid element when, situated at a height of
some thirty degrees to the west at nightfall, that star is about to vanish
in the wake of the sun. There is, then, a homological relation between
the vertical thread that is believed to come out of the spider's anus and
the rain coming out of "Juya's hole" (thread : spider :: rain : Juya). The
language tends to confirm this connection, since in Guajiro the word
for "anus" is *asio'u*, or *eio'u*, literally "the hole in the tail."

But how then are we to explain the variant in which Calabash takes
the place of spider? The calabash (*ita*) is the receptacle most commonly
used by the Guajiro to hold drinking water, which it inevitably suggests
to them:

Before, the Guajiro used to carry their *ita* with them.
It was always in the small bag hanging from their belts.

Thus, wherever they were, they could have water. The elders still do it.

Now, for the Guajiro, the best drinking water is rainwater, "Juya's water": when heavy storms occur, many Guajiros construct a complex system of gutters and receptacles to collect it.

In both cases, then, this episode indirectly signifies the transformation of men into rain, a transformation that takes place after they have passed over to the realm-beyond-death, into Juya's domain.[31] For in returning to earth, the hero of the myth causes the intercession of "carriers" who are true metaphorical representations of the rain. Likewise, the long-dead Indians are responsible for the rains that water the earth:

hero of the myth : carrier :: a person long dead : rain

Here again this shows that when they associate men with the rains or with *wanülüs*, the Guajiro are not referring to a genuine transformation of men into rains or *wanülüs*. The relation is hazier, more abstract, at once expressing and justifying their ambivalent attitude toward the dead and, ultimately, toward death: by associating it, on the one hand, with the rain, which is necessary and beneficial, they attenuate its absurdity; by associating it, on the other, with disease, they justify its presence on earth, constantly made manifest.[32]

The Sojourn on Earth

(On earth the hero meets up again with his mother and sister, who weep and make him talk. By recounting his adventure he places himself in the situation of a dead man. The Guajiro Orpheus dies. Lines 480–509.)

By stating in conclusion that it is not possible for human beings to escape their destiny, the myth clearly shows that its function is not to propose illusory solutions but solely to explore and to instruct.

It should also be noted that the first part of the reference myth may be said to be an inversion of the last episode: by his tears the man had caused his wife to come back from the land of the dead; by the tears of his sister and mother he is finally sent back there. It would be tempting to seek an explanation for this episode that would involve Guajiro kinship relations, which are often characterized by a violent latent opposition between the members of the husband's lineage and those of the wife's lineage. But the existence of a variant recounting the story of a man weeping for his dead brother before returning to see him in Jepira (above, pp. 102–104) shows that this opposition, while significant, is not fundamental.

We have now come to the end of an itinerary that, by taking us through myths and rites, has enabled us to apprehend certain Guajiro conceptions of death, appreciate their logic, and also better understand some of the practices associated with them. Throughout this analysis the concepts of Juya and Pulowi have lighted our way, together with the categories they have made it possible to define.

Setting aside for a moment the Guajiro conception of death, I shall next show that they underlie many other social practices and many other beliefs.

4. *Sükuaitpa Wayu Alaüla:* The Custom of the Old Guajiros

When they observe certain rites or give expression to certain beliefs and customs, the Guajiro justify them simply by referring to "the custom of the elders," *sükuaitpa wayu alaüla.*

Among the Guajiro the relations between rites or beliefs and myths are not explicit as they often seem to be in other societies. Apparently there is no direct, manifest relationship between their ritual practices and their world view, built up as it were around the mythical beings Juya and Pulowi.

Juya and Pulowi are the subject of no prayer, no cult, no sacrifice. But at a second level they reveal themselves in rites and beliefs, through the symbolic constructs referred to in the foregoing pages. A few examples are in order here.

Rain Rituals

Toward the end of the dry season the Indians of Upper Guajira perform a ritual that consists in filling in the holes dug out by certain iguanids. These holes, they say, stop the rain from falling (see Part One, lines 7049–8013). People forgather, assemble all that remains in the way of food, and organize a celebration, *emi'ira*, in the course of which the men block the holes made by the reptiles with earth, stones, or even rubbish. How is this practice to be explained?

It will be remembered that reptiles are associated with Pulowi. Blocking the openings to the tunnels that some of them dig in the earth stops them from coming out and thus removes from the surface of the earth elements opposed to Juya. This interpretation is confirmed by certain Guajiros who say that this rite is performed "to stop Pulowi from getting out" (cf. lines 7097–7098).

A Diviner Who Makes the Rain Fall

Here follow some extracts from an account given by an old female shaman:

> In Upper Guajira
> at the foot of a mountain where my son-in-law lived
> it had not rained for a long time
> and the cattle were dying because of the drought.

So the people living there called in a clever diviner.
The man climbed up the mountain.
He stopped halfway up and started divining.
"Down there, under that pile of earth, there's a snake.
She is very big. I can hear her growling and shaking.
It's because of her that it has stopped raining!"
said the diviner.
The men gathered a lot of wood
and piled it up on the spot designated by the diviner.
Then they set it alight.
"*Chuaaa . . . tsü!*" they heard from amid the flames.

The next day, in the burnt earth, under a rock,
they saw an enormous hole.
That was where the snake lived.

Now it rains a great deal there
and the people are very rich.

Before the diviner came
a man had gone on the mountain where the snake lived.
When he came back the man dropped dead.
He dropped dead because that place was *pulowi*.

(Recounted by Reachon Aapshana on September 18, 1973. This woman,
aged about eighty, is a shaman at Piruachon, in Venezuelan Guajira.)

Throughout the peninsula comparable stories are related. They are
governed by the same logic as the rain rituals considered above. To state
that a snake lives inside the mountain where it does not rain is to associate the snake with drought (and with death), which is a characteristic of the *pulowi* principle. To kill the snake is to eliminate that principle, opposed to the rain (and to life).

The Rainbow and the Reptiles

It is worth recalling here the explanation given by the Guajiro for the
rainbow: they say that it comes out of the mouth of snakes or certain
reptiles (lines 8029–8041, 8047–8049). I have already emphasized and
partly accounted for this connection between the rainbow and reptiles
by introducing the opposition between rain and drought in Chapter 2,
which may be recalled briefly. The rainbow is sporadically opposed to
the rain as the dry season is opposed to the wet season. To account for
the origins of the rainbow, the Guajiro make reference to one of the representations of Pulowi. By the same token they assert that rain and rainbow are complementary and both necessary, as are Juya and Pulowi
their counterparts. "Without rainbow, it would rain continually," they
say: without Pulowi, Juya would be excessively present.

Ka'ulayawakat, the "Festival of the Goat"

When the September rains were plentiful and gave promise of a rich harvest, the Guajiro engaged in long celebrations known as *ka'ulayawakat*—literally, "doing the goat." This practice, which seems to have been very widespread a few decades ago, has now become very rare, apparently because of the change in economic practices brought about by the development of the markets in the border regions. This festival, which lasted for several weeks or months, was an occasion for large gatherings and was accompanied by collective agricultural work now fallen into disuse. A number of Guajiros experience real pleasure or great nostalgia now when they talk about the *ka'ulayawa*, of which they gave me many detailed descriptions.

In particular, during that festival a large number of games of a theatrical and competitive nature were organized, led by singers who determined the tempo and order of the events.

One of them represents a combat between "cloud and *wanülü*": *atkashi wanülü süma siruma*, literally "*wanülü* fights with cloud." It consists in a contest between two men, one representing a cloud, the other a *wanülü*. Ideally the game should end with the victory of the cloud. Although the connection does not appear to be recognized consciously by the Guajiro, there can be no clearer illustration of the opposition between Juya and Pulowi, "represented" respectively by cloud and *wanülü*. It should be noted in addition that, in urging the symbolic victory of the cloud, the Guajiro display their optimism and reaffirm their confidence: the rain always manages the triumph over the drought, life finally vanquishes disease and death.

Another game is called the combat of "the sea against the water," *atkasü palaya süma wüin*. The water here is that which, on the occasion of the sudden floods that come in the wake of heavy rainfall, races into the sea. The players split up into two equal groups. Standing in lines, back to back, they try to push one another back. "It's always the water that wins; those representing the sea must let the others get the best of them," say some Guajiros. Here is an example in which a simple natural phenomenon assumes a highly symbolic significance. It is not merely the confrontation of the water of the rivers in spate and the water of the rising tide that is expressed by this ritual game. For it does not have such great importance in Guajiro life. If this phenomenon has been chosen, it is because it too is homologous with the couple formed by Juya and Pulowi: the sea represents the *pulowi* principle, the rainwater the *juya* principle.

The Seasons and the Stars

Likewise, the logic revealed by analysis of the myths throws some light on the Guajiro Indians' "system of seasons." Or, to be more prudent and more precise, its application to this area reveals certain peculiarities that may perhaps be confirmed by future investigations.

The Guajiro divide the year into "seasons," which they enumerate in a definite order, as we do with our months, with the difference that the length of each season is not constant. In addition, as has already been stressed, they make a close connection between the apparent course of the stars and these divisions of the year, since the same word (e.g., *iiwa*) or two very similar words (e.g., *juyo'u* and *juya*) designate equally the star (or the constellation) and the associated season.

But certain seasons do not seem to have corresponding stars or constellations. They are defined by the appearance of relatively irregular phenomena such as the flowering of plants or certain changes in vegetation, or they are associated with wild animals. For instance, *patsuasi*, literally "flower of *patsua*," and *uraichisia*, "blossoming of the *uraichi*," are said to begin at the first appearance of flowers on those trees. *Pshalesüin*, "drink of the falcon," is said to correspond to that bird's nest-building period. Similarly, *iramasüin* derives from *irama* (deer), *waliriyu* from *walirü* (fox), and so forth.

Are these two types of seasons distributed haphazardly through the year or, on the contrary, do they follow one another in a specific order? In Figure 2 Guajiro seasons are set in parallel with our months.[1] The diagram thus obtained immediately reveals that the stars which define the seasons are divided into two groups. One is centered on Arcturus (*juyo'u*), which defines the "midpoint" of the main rainy season, and the other on the Pleiades (*iiwa*), the "midpoint" of the short wet season. Between these two groups are two spaces not marked by the presence of stars. These correspond to the dry seasons, extending from mid-December to the end of March and from mid-June to mid-September. For further confirmation the reader may look at the curves representing the average rainfall during the year (Chapter 2, note 3). In these intervals the names of the seasons derive from the names of wild plants or animals.

For this peculiarity one is tempted to put forward an explanation based on the general logic developed throughout this study. For the names designating the stars also refer to mythical beings. In the traditional tales these superhuman beings, such as Iiwa, Oummala, and Iruala, help Juya in his expeditions against Pulowi (e.g., lines 624–633). Like Juya they are regarded as unique, male beings in perpetual movement—"the stars walk (*waraitshi*)," say the Guajiro. They take turns with him, to rain or to send lightning. "They are the rains," *juyakanü*. Wild plants and animals, on the contrary, are linked to Pulowi.

The two types of Guajiro seasons and their distribution in the year would appear, then, to reflect the logical system that associates Juya with the rains and stars and Pulowi with drought and wild plants or animals.

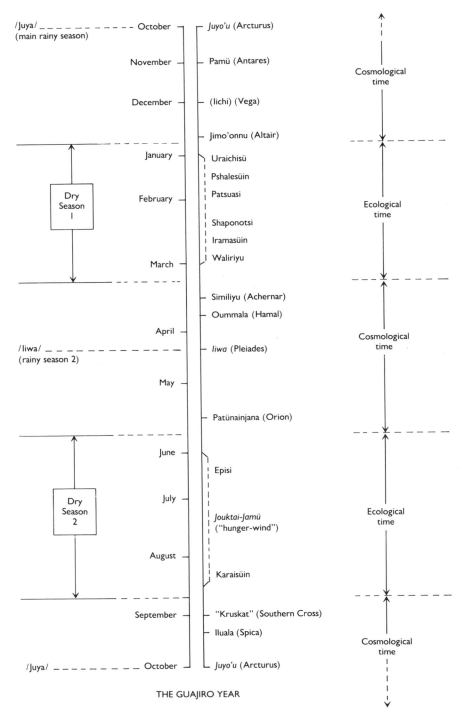

Figure 2. (Italics indicate "key names," used as references by the Guajiro.)

But as attractive as this interpretation may be, its dubiousness should not be disguised. For the indifference and ignorance of most Guajiro today as regards astronomical matters make it difficult to pursue this line of inquiry. The data are largely derived from averages, and of some thirty names of seasons communicated to me, only about half are shown on the chart in the absence of satisfactory information.[2]

The Yonna Dance and the Prescriptions of the Shamans

The *yonna* dance, known in Venezuela and Colombia by the name *chicha maya*, is undoubtedly a very popular and commonly practiced form of community event among the Guajiro today.

The pretexts for organizing a *yonna* dance are as varied as they are numerous. It commemorates happy events like marriages, the beginning or end of the period of a girl's seclusion, economic successes, and so on. It is offered as a token of esteem on the occasion of visits by important individuals. But above all, it is frequently prescribed by the shamans in accordance, so they say, with the wishes of their *spirits*, who demand it to ensure the return of the *soul* and the complete recovery of their patients. The *yonna* dance is the main opportunity for the members of a local group living in highly scattered settlements to come together for a few hours or one or two days. Always accompanied by the distribution of food and drink offered by the small group organizing it, it forms part of a cycle of economic services and exchanges. Here, however, we shall consider only its symbolic value.

The *yonna* dance takes place near the host's house, on an ordinary flat and bare area of land, cleared beforehand of any rubbish or objects that might hurt the dancers' feet. This dance floor (*piouy*) is roughly circular and measures an average of ten to fifteen meters across. The movements are executed by a couple to the beat of a drum. (See Photographs 18 and 19.) The man's face is painted and he wears a plumed crown. Called *karatsü*, this headdress is now worn solely on the occasion of this ceremony. The woman, whose face is also painted but with other motifs, wears a very long shawl known as *ko'usü*, or *pannerü ko'usü*, literally "the cloth with a hole in it," which goes over her head and descends all the way to the ground. The man retreats before the woman, who advances on him with quick short steps and tries to make him fall down. Her arms opened out, the woman holds her shawl taut with her two hands; at the same time she also holds the two sides of her dress, which gives her from both the front and back a very elegant diamond-shaped silhouette. The male dancer eggs on his partner by shouting, "*Josei! püsaja emirua! Josei! püsaja emirua!*": "Go and get your younger sister!" (if, that is, you cannot make me fall . . .). The women take turns until the man falls to the ground or admits to being tired. In the first eventuality, the fall is accompanied by enthusiastic shouts and jeers from the spectators gathered around the dancing area. Another man then comes and takes his place or a new couple goes onto the floor. On an average, one man dances consecutively with three or four female dancers.

The *yonna* dance mimes a genuine struggle between man and woman. In this it clearly caricatures the Guajiro couple, with several women taking turns to attack and knock over the man, who is unique and irreplaceable. But over and above this trivial representation, this dance possesses a deeper symbolic significance. At the end of my first investigation I felt this intuitively without being able to demonstrate it. In the course of a second period of field research, in the light of the results of my analysis of the mythology, I was able to collect proof in support of this hypothesis.

The monochrome facial paintings (*achepü* or *achepia*)[3] with which the dancers adorn themselves vary according to sex. The designs reserved for men are composed mainly of segments of straight lines (*shawatüin*, "it is straight, it is standing"), while the women's designs, far more complex, consist chiefly of curves (*oskokonojushi*, or *lakalakalin*, "it is curved") between which dots (*iwa'uya*) may be inserted. Each motif has a distinct name. Generally speaking, the participants seem free to choose any one of the motifs provided that it belongs to their sex.

But when the dance is prescribed by shamans, at the end of a cure or following a dream, it is they who impose the design. It then becomes apparent that they nearly always ask the dancers to paint two single motifs on themselves: *jerüi'chepuya* for the women and *juya'saya* for the men. The first term means "like the painting of the *jerüi*." The word *jerüi* designates a long, thin snake that, although not poisonous, is greatly feared by the Guajiro. They claim that this snake can kill them by penetrating their ears or any other natural opening and that it is particularly liable to attack pregnant women, causing them to miscarry. To achieve its ends, it "produces a wind that enables it to fly": *kojouktaishüsü wüikat jerüi*, literally "he has a wind the snake *jerüi*." The term *juya'saya* is the contracted form of the expression *nüsaya Juya*, which means "like the legs of Juya."

Thus Pulowi, signified by the *jerüi* snake, is closely associated with the woman dancer. Juya is clearly associated with the male dancer. The dancing couple represents, so to speak, the superhuman couple formed by Juya and Pulowi. Hence shamans give to the *yonna* dance a clear symbolic meaning. This is not surprising considering the important role played by Guajiro shamans in safeguarding and transmitting traditional "mythical thought" insofar as they consolidate beliefs and rituals by constantly, in their diagnoses and their interpretations of dreams and occurrences, availing themselves of a way of thinking in which everything—people, animals, plants, acts, and things—can take on essentially a metaphorical significance.

The style of dress of the two dancers furnishes proof of the validity of this symbolic interpretation of the *yonna* dance. The *karatsü* (or *kialüjü*) headdress worn by the male dancer (and sometimes the drum player) is made of a woven crown (*kotsü*) and an "arm" (*stüna*) made of several ara or cock feathers or sometimes the tail of a fox. This arm is attached to the crown by means of a regular binding of polychrome threads (*sülaja*, "the fastening"). Some Guajiros compare this fastening with Jolotsü, the planet Venus, or with Juyo'u, the star Arcturus (Fig. 3).

The *karatsü* would seem, then, to represent Juya with his eye (the fastening) and his single arm (the tuft of feathers), in the same way as Arcturus and the constellation of stars that link it to the Great Bear represent him in the night sky.[4] More loosely but no less clearly, the dress of the woman, who through the "hole" in her shawl allows her face to be barely glimpsed, may be said to symbolize the subterranean, hidden, shadowy figure of Pulowi.

The Pregnant Woman and the Snakes

The Guajiro assert that it is dangerous for a pregnant woman to meet a snake. Inadvertently to walk over one results in a miscarriage. This danger has just been referred to in connection with the *jerüi* snake, which has acquired a particularly bad reputation on this account.

Consulted immediately after such an occurrence, a shaman may propose a treatment designed to ward off the evil. Thus, one of them asked the parents of the victim to go immediately in search of a snake of the same species as that seen by the pregnant woman, to kill it, and carefully to open its belly in order to find there, "in a kind of pouch, the water it had absorbed." This had then to be recovered and brought to the patient, who at once swallowed it. By means of this treatment "the miscarriage was prevented and the baby was delivered without any problem."[5]

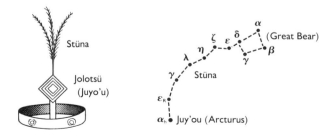

Figure 3. Left, the *karatsü* crown; right, "the eye and arm" of Juya in the night sky.

There is a striking analogy between the snake and its "water pouch" and the amazing combat waged by the "small calabash" against the snake of the Pulowi of Ayajui (lines 598–602), a combat that, as can now be easily seen, also illustrates the fundamental opposition between Juya and Pulowi since, as we saw, the calabash may stand for Juya and the snake may be a "mobile substitute" for Pulowi. Did this episode of the myth provide the shaman with the basis for his prescription? No final answer can be given, of course, to this direct question. But one may legitimately wonder what logic he was more or less consciously obeying when he formulated his prescription.

According to our analysis, snake means sickness, danger, death. It therefore presents a threat to the pregnant woman, the promise and symbol of a new and still precarious life, to which it is logically opposed. Any encounter with it must then be avoided. To kill the snake and to extract from it the principle that is symbolically opposed to it—water, the principle of life—is to modify the relations of the opposing terms and to give life every chance against death (miscarriage).

It is interesting to note here that the snake—although essentially on the side of Pulowi—is marked under such circumstances by two contradictory but complementary principles (life-death), as is every aspect of reality according to the Guajiro. It is but a "weakened" expression of the *pulowi* principle.

The reader, attentive to this "ritual medication," will not have failed to note in this connection a strange paradox of Guajiro thought. On the one hand, it associates woman with Pulowi, the symbol of death, but on the other, it has to come to terms with her procreative function. The following three studies throw further light on this ambiguous position occupied by Guajiro women, since they deal with facts of very close concern to them: the seclusion of girls, shamanism, and the organization of society into clans. But these studies will be less stringent than the previous ones and based on less proof. Why then include them here? Because, with the study of the symbolic dimension of such social practices—which are present in a large number of societies and whose underlying significance is clearly not to be sought in purely intellectual terms—we come to the field of pure ideology and reinterpretation, thereby marking the boundaries of this analysis.

The Guajiro Girl's Period of Seclusion

When she attains puberty a Guajiro girl, called *jimo'olu*, is subjected to a period of seclusion—*süttüsü paülü*, or *shükonolüsü*[6]—at the end of which she has become a *majayülü*, a marriageable young woman. Nowadays this custom is still observed, but the Guajiro greatly stress the fact that this stage in a woman's life is shorter and milder than what it used to be "in the olden days." The period of seclusion could, according to the girl's social position, be as much as five years among the richest Indians. Nowadays it lasts an average of three to eight months. The beginning of this period coincides with the first menstruation.⁷ The girl's hair is then cut short and she is installed in a hammock very high up, close to the roof of the house: *majayüchon kachetüsü ipüna sulu süi.* She is shielded from other people's gaze by a piece of cloth stretched out beneath her hammock. In theory she must neither move nor eat nor drink for three to five days. She is then delivered (*ashakatünüsi*, literally "she has come down"), and her mother, sometimes helped by close kinswomen, bathes her and makes sure that she has remained "well closed," that is, virginal (*shasü*). The family sometimes organizes a *yonna* dance to celebrate the event. But the girl, shielded from people's gaze, does not participate. She begins her long seclusion during which she will acquire a mastery of women's work, weaving, spinning, and so on, instructed by her mother, her grandmother, or other close kinswomen. In theory she must neither be seen by men nor attempt to see them. Formerly the secluded girl used to live in a small separate house, called *shükona*, built specially for that purpose. The entrance to that dwelling was narrow and low, sometimes closed with a piece of material or cowhide (*sta pa'a*). It was difficult to enter it and impossible to see inside. Nowadays it is very seldom used. The *shükona* now takes the form of pieces of hanging cloth demarcating an "isolated space" within the collective dwelling. The end of the period of seclusion is marked by a *yonna* dance to which kinfolk, neighbors, allies, and friends are invited. This is the occasion for presenting in public the young woman ready for marriage.

The Guajiro account for this custom in a variety of ways. Its primary purpose, they say, is to "take away the girl's unruly spirit"—*suliejat mujuin shki*, to make her well behaved—*ka'injüjat*, literally "to put *soul* (*a'in*) into her." Others assert that if she were not secluded, the girl would never have the healthy, firm body of Guajiro women, that she would age rapidly. Finally, as the "whiteness of a woman's skin" (*kasutat, kasutalüin*) is a quality highly appreciated by Guajiro men, this consequence of seclusion is, in the eyes of some, enough to explain it; moreover, seclusion is sometimes called *akasujuna*, "to be whitened."

But this practice can be considered in a different light on the basis of the lessons drawn from the myths: the secluded girl could be a metaphorical representation of Pulowi. Having to acquire the maximum "femininity" (*jierüin shia*) with a view to marriage, she can be regarded as metaphorically taking the place of that mythical being by remaining "hidden indoors" and going out only at nighttime—to relieve herself—unseen by anyone. Neutralized by marriage, she is subsequently considered to have departed from this "zenith."

Indeed, there are other cases in Guajiro society of people being forced into seclusion—initiation of shamans, isolation of murderers, and so on—that are not related to Pulowi. In the case of girls, however, certain facts suggest that the Guajiro implicitly establish a connection. Girls who remain in seclusion are referred to as *pülainrü* (see Chapter 2, "The Meanings of Words") and are regarded as *pülasü*, that is, dangerous, taboo, and related to the supernatural world. This provides linguistic evidence of the link between Pulowi, the very *pülasü* supernatural woman, and the secluded girl. The countless myths that portray Pulowi as a young woman always living "inside her house" also support this interpretation.[8]

The Majority of Guajiro Shamans Are Women

According to my estimates, the proportion of men to women among Guajiro shamans is one to seven. Furthermore, even when their medical abilities are recognized, male shamans are often regarded, rightly or wrongly, as homosexuals. Some ethnologists have seen in this female predominance, rare in Amerindian shamanism, the mark of strong European influence in that society.[9] This interpretation is of course plausible, but this peculiarity can also be seen as a reflection of the Guajiro system of mythical thought. It is obviously not possible to prove that there exists a causal relationship between the feminization of shamanism and this symbolic system. But it is clear that this system has been applied to shamanism and that the entire ideology developed around this practice proceeds from it.

Let us consider the following extract from the remarks of a woman shaman stressing the close relationship she is supposed to have with Pulowi:

We the shamans, we know Pulowi.
Our *spirit, washeyukot,* meets her
in that *pulowi* place where the souls of the sick are prisoners.
And to go and get them back,
there where we go,
we turn into Pulowi:
pülouitkaka waya.

Similarly, it will be recalled that shamans commonly call their *spirits* by the name of *wanülü*, thereby marking this closeness to disease and death that they must always maintain (see above, pp. 82–83). What could be more normal, then, than preferring a shaman of the female sex, symbolically on the side of Pulowi, so that the "distance to be covered" to "find" the sickness (*wanülü*) is shorter and easier to cross, so to speak, or attributing to the male shaman a real or invented femininity?

Certain aspects of the life of Guajiro shamans are bound to strengthen this bond with Pulowi. The Guajiro say that girls who later become shamans have in many cases remained secluded for a longer period than is usual, and many assert that they have almost all been *pülainrü* girls and "that it is better thus":

Maimajeya pülainrüin outsükaleiru.
Many shamans are *pülainrü.*
They grow old without having husbands,
but it would be dangerous for them to marry.
Tü piachika pülasü ma'i toloyu, ouktüsü:
To female shamans men are fatal,
they die because of them.

In actual fact, most women shamans are married, but they must, so they insist, have limited sexual relations with their husbands, just as if, to remain close to Pulowi, they needed to avoid the "neutralization" resulting from marriage:

Our husbands are our *spirits*, our *wanülüs*,
and they would kill us if we stayed long with another man.

This is not the place to go further into the study of Guajiro shamanism, a complex field calling for special analysis. But it seems worthwhile emphasizing this convergence of an original and purely speculative body of thought and a practice whose general principles, on the contrary, are shared by many other Amerindian societies.

All the rites, customs, and beliefs that we have just examined confirm the logical pattern of Guajiro mythical thought insofar as it explains or justifies them through recourse to analogies between the terms of each of two opposing series. For instance, from the Guajiro standpoint, there is a symbolic equivalent between death, drought, below, snake, Pulowi, or between life, rain, mobility, above, Juya.

But between the mythical universe and the social world of the Guajiro there exist more formal correspondences.

The Myth of the Origin of Human Beings and Clans

Here is how the origin of the Guajiro Indians and their matriclans is recounted in a variant of the very long myth relating the birth and life of the demiurge Maleiwa:

Maleiwa went to Wotkasainru,
a clayey land, in Upper Guajira.
He then took some clay to make human beings.
He molded much earth
and he fashioned figurines that resembled people.
"These are the ones who will speak!" he said.
He then fashioned figurines that resembled cattle
to give to the rich Guajiros who would own them.
Starting from tracks, he made the marks of the clans.[10]

One mark for the Uliana,
one mark for the Jayaliyu.
One mark for the Uraliyu,
one mark for the Sapuana.
One mark for the Iipuana,
one mark for the Jitnu . . .
And he distributed the cattle.
In the men's hands he placed weapons,
knives, machetes, spades . . .

Then Maleiwa divided up the Guajiro,
like dividing up sheep as they come out of a paddock:
one here, one there . . .
He led each one to his or her designated land.

This is why the Guajiro can now say
where the ancestors of their clans were born.

But when they refer more specifically to the ancestors of their own clan, the Guajiro more readily recount the following story:

Each Guajiro clan has its land.
In that land is the hole where our ancestors emerged:
ko'usü chaya tü ma sujutüin weki.
Two Jayaliyus emerged at Tapuli,
a man and a woman.
From over there come the ancestors of that clan.
Two Pushainas emerged at Aulechi,
a man and a woman.
Over there is the hole where the ancestors of the clan come from.
Two Iipunas emerged at Se'epana,
a man and a woman.
Two Uraliyus emerged at Katainsü.
Two Jitnus emerged at Talwayupana . . .

The first myth asserts that the Guajiro were made by Maleiwa from clay in the same locality of Guajira. According to the second, each clan emerged from the earth through holes whose whereabouts are now known to the Guajiro. This contradiction does not escape the Indians, but they are willing to assume it since one of the myths enables them firmly to express their allegiance to a specific culture and the other equally strongly their attachment to the clan.

What is chiefly to be noted here is the parallel between this "representation" of social organization and the way in which the *pulowi* principle is given expression. The Guajiro describe the holes through which the clans emerged in the same way as *pulowi* places:

The Aapshana came out over there
from between the stones,
through a hole in the ground.

Komochojülü is a *pulowi* place.
Between the stones there is a hole in the ground.
It is through there that Pulowi comes out.

Is this parallel a merely superficial one or does it conceal a deeper meaning? It may be thought to, considering that, just as the clan system perpetuates the "flesh" of Guajiro society (*eiruku*, "clan," also means "flesh"), so Pulowi also assumes responsibility for it by parsimoniously distributing the game whose survival it is her function to ensure. Light might thus be shed on the strange femininity of Pulowi and, incidentally, on the ambiguous position of the Guajiro woman, mentioned above. The giver of death at the individual level, Pulowi would thus be indirectly responsible for social reproduction, like the clan. At the same time, the Guajiro woman would be thought of primarily at the social level: more as the one who ensures the clan's continuation than as a begetter. It is perhaps for this reason that there is nothing today more marked by confusion and contradiction than Guajiro ideas about human reproduction, a subject that the Indians seem loathe to discuss.[11]

This link between the clans and *pulowi* might also partly provide the key to the fact that an animal is associated with each matrilinear clan: since Pulowi is first and foremost the "mistress of the animals," it would be logical to establish a correspondence between all the clans and all the animals.

But, in advancing these two hypotheses, I have already departed from what can be demonstrated and am dealing with conjecture.

5. A Vanishing Civilization?

At the time of the West's intrusion it seems likely that the Guajiro lived from hunting and fishing, horticulture and food gathering. Guajiro society must therefore have experienced a long period of instability as the practice of stock breeding spread throughout the Indian zone. This economic upheaval led to changes in social structure, but how fast these occurred and on what scale it is difficult to know in the absence of sufficiently precise observations throughout this "historical" period.[1] However, it is possible to form an idea of the nature of these changes by now studying in various regions of the peninsula the increasingly marked deviations between the norms still voiced by the Guajiro and their actual practices. A modification of the rules of matrilocal residence is thus revealed with the appearance of avunculocality and even patrilocality, and the disintegration of the classical matrilinear system is seen. Similarly, new forms of inheritance appear, with a tendency to recognize dual filiation or even implicitly to obey a rule of patrilinear filiation. What is the situation as regards the more sheltered domain of oral literature and "things of the mind"?

The reader will not have failed to notice that stock breeding is of secondary importance in the stories so far included in this book. Cattle often form part of the background against which they take place but they rarely play an active role. These myths give the impression that hunting has remained the main economic activity of the Guajiro. Despite this manifest attachment to tales of which the heroes are hunters and fishermen, however, certain myths give evidence of an attempt to "move with the times."

In an earlier text we saw, for instance, a herdsman in a role traditionally assigned to a hunter ("The Pulowi of Matujai," Part One, lines 884–928). Other tales which I shall not quote here show how Pulowi swallows a herd at the same time as its keeper or uses as messenger a huge bull or a snake with a cow's head (see also lines 2047–2052). But there also exist myths wholly devoted to cattle, namely those raising the problem of their origin. One tells, for example, how the horse appeared to a Guajiro in the form of a colt and asked him to domesticate it. Another explains how the cows emerged one day from the sea, together with the goats and sheep. It is hardly worth including them here, but it should be stressed that they seem designed to show above all that the *alijunas*, the white foreigners, lie when they claim to have given cattle to the Guajiro:

Cows, sheep, goats . . . ,
they do not come from elsewhere, as the *alijunas* assert.
Where would they have been brought from?
All Guajiro cattle come from this land where we live!
Those who claim that they come from elsewhere tell lies.
Deer, where do they come from?
Rabbits, where have they been sent from?
All that is found here was here before.

And yet it was at the beginning of the sixteenth century that the first head of cattle were brought from Europe to this northern region of South America. And around 1550, according to the chroniclers, some Guajiros had already accumulated livestock by means of raids or theft:

They discovered broad savannahs
covered in cacti and thorns,
inhabited by inhuman folk
called in that region *cocinas*
with legs so light and slender
they resemble those of the deer.
They saw an abundance of rabbits and deer
and a large quantity of cattle.

(Juan de Castellanos, *Elegias de varones ilustres de Indias.* This text describes a journey made to the northwest of the peninsula in 1559.)

THE SOJOURN IN SUN'S DOMAIN

There does not exist, nor ever will exist, a community or a group of communities whose mythology and ethnography can be known in their entirety. The ambition to achieve such knowledge is meaningless, since we are dealing with a shifting reality, perpetually exposed to the attacks of a past that destroys it and of a future that changes it.

(C. Lévi-Strauss, *The Raw and the Cooked*)

But apart from banal substitutions or new founding myths that have, however, little of value to offer, some rare but highly interesting examples of tales are to be found that give proof of an effort to interpret and analyze new material with the help of the traditional system of thought. The following tale is an outstanding example of these.

KA'I AND PULOWI

Esü wane wayu washirü, jierüinja shia . . .
There was a rich Guajiro woman.
She owned many horses,
many cows,
many sheep, many goats . . .

She had a large number of peons
but she did not watch over them.
Her thirsty horses wandered here and there.
If they went near a waterhole
the drunken peons hit them.
They threw stones at them.

Eka wane ama paruta, majulashi . . .
Among the horses there was a very wayward stallion.
He tormented the others.
At nighttime he led them away in small groups
to an unknown place.

"My horses are disappearing!
Go and look for them!" said the woman.
The peons scoured all the lands
but they did not find them.
Nowhere did they hear speak of them.
No one had seen them.
The following days other horses got lost.
Very few now remained.

The woman then attended to them herself.
She tied up those that remained.
She hobbled them.
She was very fond of her stallion
but she decided to sell him.
He was very handsome, very big,
and the *alijunas* had always wanted to buy him.
She exchanged him for ten mares.
"Don't untie him for he is a wayward one!
He might go off far away," she said.

The next day no horses disappeared, nor the following days.
But later
when the woman had already stopped thinking of him,
the stallion got loose.
He arrived near the horses at the end of the evening.
The next day they had all broken their ropes.
Not a single one was left.
The stallion had come to let them loose.

The woman set off at dawn
following their tracks.
Their hoof marks led her far away;
then she could no longer see them.
They had vanished in shifting, muddy ground,

effaced by the countless tracks
of bitterns and *junuunais*. [2]
She stayed alone there
without eating for two days.
She wanted to disappear.
She wept . . .

Nantaka wane wayu washirü sünainmüin, mulauchi . . .
A rich Guajiro then came along,
riding a mule.
"What are you doing here?" he asked.
"I'm looking for my horses."
"What has happened to them?"
"They have run away.
For four days I have been looking for their tracks.
Müliasü a'in taya! I am very unhappy!"
"I'm sorry for you," said the man.
"But did you love your horses or did you make them suffer?"
"Why would I have come looking for them here
if I did not love them?"
"If you want to see them, I'll show them to you,"
said the man.
"I want to see them!"
"Then let's go!"

The woman followed the Guajiro.
They came to a big door.
The door opened by itself.
The woman at once saw a paddock and the man's house.
There were cows, horses, sheep . . . ,
and many waterholes.
"Hurry up!" said the man.
On the way he spoke to her.
"Did you see your horses?" he asked.
"Yes! Over there are those that went missing first!"
The woman also saw her horses that had long been dead.
They were in a separate paddock.
"Follow me! Let's hurry off to see your horses!"

"Now you stay here!" said the man.
Joulika taya ayatashi, no joyshi taya jimatüin!
"I have to work, I can't keep still!
But be careful!
This house is my wife's
and my wife is bad.
Don't go and look at her! Don't move from here!

She'll try to make you come,
to make you talk.
To do that, she'll change form.
Even if strange things occur
stay here, do not look!
Here there is water.
You may drink if you are thirsty.
Here is your food!"
The man gave her some corn and cheese.
There were only very small pieces,
but there was enough to fill her up.
She had very little water,
but she could not finish it.
A very small drop was enough to slake her thirst.
The man took her to the place where she was to sleep.
"I'm going off now.
I'll come back when I have to," he said.

He whom the woman saw going off now was the sun.
For the man was Ka'i, Sun . . .

He came back in the evening
when it was dark.
"How are you?" he asked her.
Sometimes he brought back a goat already grown big
or a kid that he carried on his back.
But all his animals had heads like those of the Guajiro.
Sometimes he carried a large gelded ram with a man's head,
or a large sheep with a man's head.
But he was not the one who ate them.
He brought them each day to feed his wife.
For she was *pulowi*, she had supernatural powers:
püloui jo'o tü nierüinka, pülasü.
And he, who walked unceasingly, was the sun:
ka'ikai waraitkai.

"Do you want to leave to avoid falling sick?"
Sun one day asked the Guajiro woman.
"I want to leave. I want to go back home."
"Don't worry. I'll take you back soon."

But one day, late in the afternoon,
the Guajiro woman went and looked.
She had forgotten what Sun had ordered.
At once Sun's wife released a great wind:
sujujaka shia jouktai süma.

The woman was knocked over, rolled round, dragged along.
When Sun arrived she was dead.
His wife was getting ready to eat her.

"What has happened?
Where is the Guajiro woman who was here?"
"There she is! She is dead!"
"I don't want any of that.
Since you killed her, make her live again,
or else I'll make the earth bad for you:
müjülüjüsü makat tatuma.
Sun's wife remade the Guajiro woman.
Once again she was alive.

"But I did tell you not to look!
You didn't listen to me,
so now you must leave.
You'll go alone!" said Sun.
"Your horses will stay here,
for you do not pay attention to what I say,
even when you are still in my house!"
"No! I'll take my horses.
I shall not leave without them!
Naja takuaipa amulouirai taya süma:
Too bad if I get lost!"
"Go away!
You'll take only those horses that came with the stallion.
The others will stay here."
"All right," said the woman.
Sun did not want to give her the horses that were dead.

"I'll give you your cattle,
but you must love them.
You wanted cattle, but you did not care for them.
Those who have animals love them!
You will make a special watering trough for the horses,
a special watering trough for the goats,
a watering trough for the cows,
so that your cattle multiply and love you.
For they do not like to drink the water in which they tread.
And if the donkeys are sick,
they'll pass on the sickness to the goats,
and the goats to the sheep . . .
If each has a watering trough the sickness will not spread.
Since you want cattle, this is what you must do."
Sun spoke a long time.

"Give me my horses,
I'll do what you say."
"Yes, now you can go."

At dawn Sun let the Guajiro woman out
by the door through which they had come in.
The rich Indian woman left.

Hardly had she gone through the door
than she found herself very close to where she lived.
She came from the side of the earth which lies below,
as though there was a hole in the earth:
ya atalüin wane sata makat unapüna, jotoolilü.

The woman came home with her horses.
There everyone was happy,
her mother, her maternal aunts, her peons.
They had all been looking everywhere for her.
They had followed her tracks.
They thought she was lost for ever.

Here is what the rich woman immediately had made:
a drinking trough for her sheep,
a drinking trough for her goats,
a drinking trough for her horses,
a drinking trough for her donkeys.
She had a trough made for each animal species.

(Recounted by Kashükemasü Jayaliyu on October 7, 1969.)

What is the significance of this myth, over and above its obvious edu-
cational and edifying character? By the succession of its episodes and
the topics covered, it calls to mind two tales discussed earlier: "The
Journey to the Beyond" and "Pulowi and the Deerhunter." I shall not
dwell here on the similarities but, on the contrary, bring out the significant differences.

One cannot fail to be surprised by the fact that the master of the
horses—but also the master of all domestic animals[3]—is not Pulowi
here, as might have been expected, but Sun. Far from being a pure fan-
tasy, this connection between the sun and domestic animals is an answer to the tricky problem of classification that must have arisen for the
Guajiro when this new kind of animal first appeared. The point is that
Sun, the mythical figure found here in the subterranean world, occupies an ambiguous position in Guajiro thought. On the one hand it is
given some of the characteristics of Juya, but on the other it is seen to
have features in common with Pulowi. This ambivalence ceases to be
surprising when we consider how the Guajiro describe the sun's course:

During the day the sun walks in the sky.
But in the evening he penetrates and plunges into the earth.
There he continues to walk.
The next morning he comes out again on the other side.

During the daytime the sun is on high, above the ground, like Juya.
At nighttime it is underground, like Pulowi. A few myths among the
rare ones in which Sun is the hero confirm this ambivalent position.
Thus one of them stresses his resemblance to Juya, recounting how he
can possess *pülainrü* women, thereby demonstrating the same "hypermasculine" character. Here are some short extracts from this myth:

There was a *pülainrü* girl.
She liked to be in seclusion.
She never went out,
not even to fetch water.

One day a sun ray entered her house,
from the roof.
Three times it came back.
The fourth day it had disappeared.

Then the girl started to get big.
She was pregnant with a son.
"I don't know what is happening to me.
No man has come to see me!" she said.

She did not think of the sun ray.
But it was Sun who was her husband.

In contrast, another story tells that Sun is the elder brother of Moon,
but also of Wanülü, affirming by this tie of kinship his nearness to Pulowi
while at the same time seeking also to emphasize what separates them:

Moon, Sun, and Wanülü are brothers:
kashikai, ka'ikai nütüma wanülü, pawalaushijaya.
Formerly they used to work together.
But one day they divided the work among themselves.
During the night
Moon, our father, works at the same time as Wanülü,
while Sun remains underground.

In what category do the Guajiro place domestic animals? For them
they are ambivalent beings partaking at once of culture and of nature.
While they are animals (*uchi*), however, they are not "products, parasites of the earth" (*she'e ma*), or "secretions of the bush" (*unapshira*),
like wild animals, but "people's animals" (*sümülüin wayu*), that is to
say, the fruit of collaboration between human beings and nature. Theo-

retically, people can do what they like with them: they can cause them to multiply, kill them, or exchange them at will. As animals they are to some extent answerable to Pulowi: although game animals are more specifically her animals—*tamülüin,* "my cattle," she says, speaking of the deer and turtles—she is commonly described in myths as the rich proprietor of two kinds of animal, the wild and the domestic. But as "cultivated products," domestic animals are on the side of Juya.[4] The richness of the pastures on which they feed depends on him, as does the size of the crops.

It is this ambivalence that is brought out by the myth when it makes Sun the master and owner of the horses and of all the cattle. The logic at work here is not difficult to understand, for we are dealing with a transformation of "The Journey to the Beyond." The couple Juya-Pulowi living on high, in Juya's domain, in the tale of the journey to the beyond has been replaced here by the subterranean couple formed by Sun and his wife, who is *pulowi* in character. The first tale, concerned with the problem of death, both used and shored up a way of thinking that, after cutting up the world into pairs of elements or opposing categories—synthesized in the mythical couple—established between them a system of correspondences. The second, having to contend with a new reality that could not easily enter into this preestablished system, found in Sun a "synthetic" mythical figure signifying this blending of opposites.[5]

At the price of what efforts, at the end of how many years, was a tale such as this created? No answers can be given to these questions. All that one can say is that it is definitely a traditional tale and not an individual creation. For I am familiar with four versions of it, recorded in different places and recounted by storytellers not connected with one another by any special relationship. Two of them are almost identical to this one. In the third, instead of horses, it is cows that disappear.

Perhaps another consequence of the ambivalence that the Guajiro attribute to domestic animals is to be seen in the belief that horses, mules, donkeys, and dogs can detect the approach of a *wanülü* or the proximity of Pulowi and are able to warn the living by means of characteristic signs: movements of the ears, cries, a refusal to advance, and so on. The story of the man who was even able to see a *wanülü* coming from afar by smearing his eyes with rheum from a dog should be recalled here. It is probably for the same reason that the Guajiro hang the skulls of horses, donkeys, sheep, or goats outside their houses or near the sunroofs and paddocks, to "keep sickness away" or to "repel *yolujas*" (Photograph 14).

This is not the place for a detailed historical account of the contacts between Guajiro society and the national societies of Colombia and Venezuela. It is worth stressing, however, two major stages in this process in order to understand better the present state of the oral literature of the Guajiro. The first stage may be said to begin with the Spanish discovery of Guajira and the first, vain attempt, in 1544, to conquer the Guajiro Indians. The second, characterized by much closer relations between Guajiros and "nationals," may be said to attest to the industrialization of Western society, the discovery of extraordinarily powerful techniques and means of communication, and a much greater desire for territorial, economic, and ideological expansion and annexation.

WANÜLÜ AND THE PRESENCE OF THE WHITES

During the first period, contacts with Western society were kept relatively well in check by the Guajiro. All the attempts at "pacification" made by Spanish troops came to grief (in 1617, 1718, 1725, etc.).[6] All the evangelizing efforts of the Franciscans, the Dominicans, and above all the Capuchins were always unsuccessful or completely undermined (in 1596, 1749, 1767, and so on). The only areas of Guajira where whites gained a lasting hold during that period were on the northern coast, where they mined salt and went after pearls with the help of Indian labor. New cultural traits appear to have made slow inroads into Indian society and, freely chosen, they had time to become well assimilated. In addition to domestic animals, this was true of the metal tools, fabrics, and strong alcoholic drinks that the Guajiro started to acquire in exchange for cattle, but also for young people sold as slaves or, on the northern coast, for their labor. Sometimes marked by violence, relations with the *alijunas* remained tense and mistrustful, localized, and kept to a minimum, although the indirect influence of the whites steadily increased. Interbreeding was rare.

We have just seen the place given to stock breeding and domestic animals in Guajiro oral literature. In the myths quoted in this book we can also appreciate the importance of certain tools inherited from the whites. We have at the same time noted the determination of the Guajiro to deny this foreign origin, a determination clearly expressed in the myth relating the origin of humans and techniques (lines 10,365–10,403) and those concerning domestic animals (p. 135 above).

But what position, what role, have the Guajiro assigned in their mythology and their symbolism to this foreigner, this *alijuna*, who, directly or indirectly, intentionally or unintentionally, has done so much to change their life? This position has long been made clear: it is that of the giver of death. We are the most common personification of *wanülü*, and we have no other recognized place (cf. lines 2075–2080, 5006–5008, 5083–5085).

It would, however, be both a simplification and an error to see in this representation no more than a direct, peremptory, and exemplary condemnation of Western civilization. The Guajiro have a far more subtly shaded attitude toward it. Indeed, their words express more often than not feelings of envy, a dramatic and irremediable sense of inferiority. This fatalistic—but not submissive—attitude is illustrated, for instance, by the now traditional amplifications of the myth of the creation of human beings (cf. "Maleiwa," Part One). Here is a short but significant version:

> At the top of the mountain Iitujulu
> Maleiwa started to mold some clay.
> He prepared a lot of earth
> and fashioned figures from which he made human beings.

> "Come!" he then said to the grandmother of the *alijunas*.
> She came at once
> without saying a word.
> Maleiwa then called the grandmother of the Guajiro.
> "Why do you make me come?" she asked him.
> Because she questioned him she remained a Guajiro.

> Maleiwa left the Guajiro a little sea and some fish,
> a little bush and some deer,
> a little cattle . . .
> "With that my grandsons will be able to eat,
> and that will suffice them!" he said.

In fact, before becoming unconsciously a sign of the implacable and murderous hegemony of the West, this close association between *wanülü* and *alijuna* was undoubtedly grounded in certain specific realities. Two main ones can be cited here. One, of a purely technical nature, is mentioned by the Guajiro themselves: the *alijuna* knows how to make weapons that are far more effective than theirs, and they have several times had occasion to judge of this effectiveness to their cost. To lend his features to *wanülü* is to give him the same deadly power and to emphasize the fatal destiny he represents. The other reality, now forgotten by the Guajiro—if, that is, they were ever consciously aware of it—is of an altogether different kind. It will be recalled that the death given by *wanülü* was generally characterized by very specific symptoms: acute, sporadic internal pains, accompanied by violent and fatal hemorrhaging. These frequently point to clear-cut cases of hemoptysis, the final stage of a form of tuberculosis often associated with cirrhosis, two diseases that, if not introduced by the whites, at least gained ten times in virulence after their arrival.

PULOWI AND TODAY'S WORLD

Since the end of the last century the national societies of Venezuela and Colombia have sent out tentacles through the whole of Guajira. Shortly after the peninsula had been shared between the two states, military posts were established in Guajiro territory, on both sides of the border.[7] Smuggling, now engaged in on a very large scale, developed apace. In 1888 some Capuchin friars provided with considerable financial resources settled in Rio Hacha, then founded the Nazaret mission in the northeastern part of the peninsula, the only one right in the heart of Indian territory. At the beginning of the century, assisted by the government, they directed the work of building a network of roads suitable for motor vehicles covering the whole of the Colombian part of the peninsula in order to "contribute to the conquest and civilization of the native of the bush." The same measures were taken by the state in Venezuelan Guajira. The "inroads of civilization" have thus multiplied at an increasingly rapid pace up to the present time. Interbreeding has become more and more common. All around the Indian territory a "buffer zone" has formed, inhabited by mestizos—generally of an Indian mother and a "Spanish" (*alijuna*) father—who, bilingual and ambitious, take advantage of the clumsy behavior of the increasingly dependent traditional Guajiros. These mestizos have organized and have a monopoly on an expensive but popular system of transport by truck throughout the peninsula. Since the establishment of official bodies whose function is to ensure "the planned transculturation and transformation of the Indian into a productive force of the nation,"[8] they serve as necessary intermediaries for sometimes inadequately trained and incompetent civil servants and misappropriate for their own purposes funds and facilities meant for the Guajiro. Finally, for more than thirty years Guajira has been drained of its lifeblood—its men. In 1949 the shantytowns of Ziruma, where emigrant Guajiros were crowded together, had to be improved by the public authorities. Since then others have formed: Los Olivos, Cujicito, and more. These suburbs of Maracaibo now house close to twenty thousand Indians.

This brief, incomplete description is sufficient to explain why—exposed to such pressure, constantly confronted with new problems, overtaken by new techniques, increasingly having to contend with the scorn and ignorance of an exploited, uneasy younger generation, fascinated by the triumphant world of industry and money—Guajiro society has not been able to come to terms with all these new developments as it had the freedom and time to do during the first period. No doubt it never will.

Today those Guajiros who have remained attached to their culture—and there are still very many of them in the older generation—are striving desperately to apply it to a world that already eludes them. Where oral literature is concerned, the result is often lame and sometimes painfully grotesque stories. We may take as examples those that seek to attest to the presence and relevance of those mythical figures who have now become familiar to us. Thus the following story, intended to prove to the incredulous the real danger still presented by Pulowi and her emissaries—if not to human beings, at least to their machines:

There was a contraband truck.
That day it was empty.
There was just the driver and his mate.

Suddenly, on the road, something glittered.
The sun was very low.
It was cold.
It was the hour when supernatural things are seen:
sütpajaka wane kasa pülain.
"What's that glittering on the road?" said the driver.
"It must be a box," replied his mate.
"No! Why would it glitter so much?"

It was a very shiny snake.
It was coming from the west, from Lumakeira.
It was going toward the east.
It was at the edge of the road.

"It's a snake!"
"Yes, it's a snake!"
"Back up! Squash it!" said the mate.
"No, that would be very dangerous.
It's not a snake, it glitters like a fire!
It's Pulowi! Leave it!"
"No! Squash it!"

The driver reversed
and he squashed the snake.
It was a very big one.
The truck had gone right over its middle.
The snake's belly was gaping open.
The men saw its entrails.
"Let's get out of here!" said the driver.

A bit further on a piece of the truck broke off.
The driver flew into a rage.
"It's because of the snake!" he said.
"Prepare for the worst!
I'm going to go back there on foot!"

When he got back there nothing remained,
only the trail of the snake,
very large.
No stain could be seen, nothing.

It was impossible to repair the truck.
It's still there.
It has been there for years,
destroyed by Pulowi.

(Recounted by Setuma Pushaina on August 13, 1973.)

Another example of this effort to apprehend a world that is getting out of control or to confirm traditional beliefs is given by this very popular tale—here again concerning Pulowi, and her emissary Wanesatai—accounting for the mysterious disappearance of a North American who came to Guajira with a companion a few years ago, probably to prospect for minerals:

The American *alijunas* worked high up in the Alaou sierra,
a very *pulowi* mountain range in Upper Guajira.
There they had built themselves a good house.
Around it they had enclosed a wide expanse of land
with barbed wire.

One day, early in the morning,
they saw a young goat coming up.

It was plump and they caught it.
They killed it, then they salted it.

The next day Wanesatai arrived: One-Limb arrived.
He had gone off in search of the goat.

He had only one leg, with the foot turned in.
He advanced waving his arms.
He was naked and his genitals could be seen.

The Americans ran off to get some trousers!
"We have a present for you!" they cried.
But Wanesatai wouldn't let them get near him.
"Take it! Take it!" the Americans shouted.
"Let's go and get a lasso,
that way we'll be able to catch him and put trousers on him!"
They set off in pursuit of him.

Before long they were in the bush.
Wanesatai was running, running . . .
One of the Americans was running behind him.
But suddenly he disappeared.

He had been swallowed up, immersed,
engulfed in the earth.
Wanesatai had taken him away with him.

The other American called and shouted,
walked up and down in every direction.
Nothing! Not a trace, not a footprint.
The next day airplanes arrived,
trucks, helicopters.
They looked everywhere, in all the mountains.
Nothing!
They couldn't find anything,
for the man was lost for ever.
Pulowi had eaten him.

(Recounted by "Andres Jose Machado" Uliyu, a stock breeder aged about
seventy, living to the west of Panasirü, in Colombian Guajira, on July 25,
1973.)

It is even related that an airplane and its pilot were swallowed by the
Pulowi of Wananai located only a few miles to the west of the mestizo
village of Paraguaipoa. This is why, according to the Guajiro, all the
searches carried out have remained fruitless and no clue has ever been
found . . .

THE END OF A WORLD?

> *Wayujaya mülou, eka jolu'u katsünaloitpa,*
> *matüjainsai so'u wane kasa.*
> *Jolu'u nojotsü shiirawain amüin kasa wayu.*
> They are adult, they wear trousers, and
> yet they are ignorant of everything.
> They don't want to know about Guajiro things.
>
> (An old man talking about
> the younger generation)

> *Yo soy un indio civilizado.*
> I am a civilized Indian.
>
> (A drunken young bilingual Indian
> wearing trousers)

"What do you know about the stars? Do you know their Guajiro
names?"
"I know *juyo'u!*"
"Can you show me it in the sky?"
"No, I can't. But the old men can! Go and ask them!"
At this burial more than a hundred people have come together. It is a

moonless, star-filled night at Pararu, near Paraguaipoa. The *foreigner* goes off to ask the old men, gathered together in the dark in tight groups. One directs an empty gaze toward the sky and scrutinizes it: "I know them all. But my eyes are so bad now that I can't see them anymore." One by one, the others confess the same incapacity. All, however, recite the names of the seasons, questioning and correcting one another.

Further on, apathetic or mocking youngsters play cards or dominoes in the light of the oil lamps or, grouped on one side, listen to music blaring from a transistor radio.

Ethnologists use the term "acculturation" (or sometimes "deculturation") to describe this loss of traditional knowledge or this refusal of ancestral wisdom resulting from contact with another civilization, generally "Western civilization." The "Guajiros who still know" have identified the origin of the malaise, of the impression of emptiness and impotence produced by this brutal rejection of a store of wisdom built up by centuries of observation and experience: the presence of the whites and the existence of the mestizos. And to express this, they desperately avail themselves of traditional modes of representation, sometimes in highly contradictory ways. Once again I shall take as an example stories about Pulowi. For some Guajiros, and particularly for the shamans, it is the gradual disappearance of Pulowi that is emphasized. Here is what a woman shaman living along a fairly busy road connecting Paraguaipoa to Kijolu (Cojoro) stated in confidence:

Now there are fewer people killed by Pulowi around here.
The shamans used to say that her victims were many.
They set traps for her.
Men stayed hidden in order to shoot arrows at *wanülüs*.
Nowadays that's less common
because there are trucks in the night,
with bright lights,
with noisy horns . . .

Wanülüs and *pulowis* have gone into hiding further up in Guajira,
further inland in the mountain regions.
Here they almost never come anymore.

One should beware, however, of interpreting this retreat of Pulowi as the sign of a notable drop in the Guajiro death rate since the establishment of a hospital at Paraguaipoa. That remains to be proved. What the old shaman is saying above all is that since the intrusion of the whites with their machines and their presumptions, the sick elude her, while at the same time the traditional culture is dying.

The modes of expression and diagnoses of the shamans no longer convince the young. For it is shamanism—a medical practice but also the cornerstone of Guajiro society—that the whites, the mestizos, and the few passing doctors attack with the greatest vehemence, without even knowing how it works or how it is practiced, taking as their justification the successes of "scientific medicine"—from which, however, they benefit very little in these remote and deprived areas.

And paradoxically, in the vain hope of consolidating their waning power, it is the shamans who open the door to the West when they attempt to "modernize" their doctrine by introducing Christian elements into it:

> *Tü aseyuwaka anaskaleiru antüsü nüma'anamüin Maleiwa:*
> Our good *spirits* go to where Christ is.
> "I've come to see the disease!" says our *spirit* to God.
> God gives our *spirit* permission to look for it.
> "You can go and see," He says.

Other tales refer, on the contrary, to a new type of Pulowi whose appearance coincided with the settling of the foreigners and the arrival of unknown ills:

> At Walakalü, near Uribia,
> lived a very large bull.
> He swallowed many Guajiros.
> Today the place where he lived is still very *pulowi.*

> Formerly there was a lot of game there,
> deer, rabbits, animals of every kind.
> Now there's nothing left.
> They've all gone back into the earth.
> It used to rain a lot.
> It no longer rains there at all.

> It's the *alijunas* who are the cause of that.
> They are clever and know how to do harm:
> *pülakaja alijunakanü.*
> All that began when they built houses
> over there, in Uribia.
> Because of the bull of Walakalü
> hundreds of Guajiros died.
> Arrows were useless against him.

There is, then, nothing very distinctive in the attitude of the Guajiro toward "Progress" and "Civilization." The old Indians talking about the old days remind one of the old people in our countrysides caught up in the same leveling movement that is sweeping away all the traditional societies of the world.

The difference is that the Guajiro will leave nothing, neither ruins nor writings to attest to their existence. And testimony to their vanishing civilization will have to be provided by the heirs of the very same one that is responsible for their annihilation. Is this a supreme demonstration of its conquering spirit or evidence of its distress before the disappearance of other possible beings, barely concealed by the "scientific attitude" or "cries of denunciation" of those who, by virtue merely of their written statements, cannot but recognize themselves as its representatives—the ethnologists?

Conclusion

Guajiro mythology, while appearing at first sight to be made up of odds and ends or remnants, has given evidence throughout these pages of an undeniable coherence.

Conducted with the greatest possible caution and stringency, the analysis has revealed essentially that a number of myths, rites, behavior patterns, and everyday acts, which appear at first glance to be unconnected with one another, have a shared structure. This is defined by a set of relations of opposition and equivalence. Simplifying somewhat, it can be said that the components of the Guajiro symbolic universe are divided into two classes of equivalence (to use a mathematical term) of which two mythical beings, Juya and Pulowi, may be regarded as the representatives and the revealers.

The small number of these classes does not make it possible to organize in any subtle way all the activities and institutions of Guajiro society. But is that their role? If an opinion had to be offered here, I would be more than inclined to say that all the forms of expression, all the sayings and doings referred to in this study, reveal and formalize the main "cultural obsessions" of the Guajiro: the dangerous mystery of female sexuality, the uneasiness of men at having to be always on the move, the necessity of women remaining immobile, the dependence on a poor and parsimonious environment, the constant anxiety concerning the severities of the climate, the fear of disease, the fatality of death. By creating a mythical universe founded on simple laws, the Guajiro defend themselves against the absurdity of their fate. By imposing an order on them, they are able to face up to the mysterious and disquieting areas of human experience.

This mythical universe is modeled on the human world. In an attempt to come to terms with obscure external forces that they cannot understand, whether in the realm of nature or in the makeup of humankind, the Guajiro have created superhuman beings. They have conferred upon them an existence similar to that of humans while investing them with higher powers. Between these beings they have imagined relationships that reflect, in an accentuated form, those that govern their society. But, in contradistinction to what happens in a large number of other cultures, these supernatural beings do not listen to humans. No word or act is explicitly addressed to them. They are first and foremost explanatory principles. And as though something had to be done to cross this unbearable gulf, the mythical structures of the Guajiro provide a link between the human world and the world of the beyond and the hidden face of things: through the intermediary of the dead, humans participate in the essence of the two principles incarnate, Juya and Pulowi, since the dead return to earth, in the form of rain or *wanülüs*, there to perpetuate life and death. The Guajiro universe is closed, cyclical, and superbly anthropocentric.

This study has shown that, while conveying the positive knowledge of a society, Guajiro oral literature expresses a distinctive conception of the world and of the problems of life. However, although it has brought to light a logic underlying the mythical thought of the Guajiros, it does not for all that make it necessary to "think like" them—far from it. For apparently the Guajiro do not possess any clear-cut awareness of the connections brought to light, and I always found the way in which they let these stories be known disconcerting. In addition, these tales never form independent wholes. In other words, not one of them exists that could be analyzed in such a way as to reveal its meaning without reference to the others. And, to discern its meaning, it is necessary to refer to an often considerable number of stories and to bring out a number of homologies. At once analytic and synthetic, Guajiro mythical thinking is seen to be synoptic, "multidimensional," as though "automatically" bringing into play equivalences and correspondences.

Why have the Guajiro not made this logical system more explicit? And why, rather than leave it incomplete and imperfect, have they not developed it—in contrast with the Dogon, for instance, who learned from their elders how to juggle interactive symbols in a world in which all that came under their observation was invested with a symbolic dimension? Has Guajiro society been maimed by history and has its mythology become, like specimens of ancient pottery, no more than scattered fragments partly reassembled by dint of laborious analysis? Or do the Guajiro not put oral literature to the same use as other peoples who are completely engrossed in their myths and for whom there is no acceptable explanation of the world that is not couched in mythical terms?

Guajiro society has, it is true, suffered a great deal of acculturation. The present period has made contacts easier and caused the traditional edifice to crumble at a faster rate. But no break has occurred in the past century. The fragments of myths quoted by one or two nineteenth-century travelers do not give any hint of a now-buried treasure trove. Is it possible, then, in an attempt to resolve the problem raised by Guajiro mythology, to put forward a hypothesis concerning the dynamic processes to which myths are subjected, concerning, that is, the relations between oral literature, society, and history?

Mythology seems caught between two requirements: that it be coherent and that it be appropriate to the real world. Starting from observable realities, social relations or relations with nature, people build themselves an imaginary universe. This universe, a product of thought, brings into play a set of parameters entering into relations of opposition, and it obeys straightforward logical rules. More or less unconsciously, this construct serves essentially to apprehend reality, that is to say, to justify phenomena and find relations between them. Of course, it also exercises an effect upon that reality of which it becomes an integral part. However, in the course of time, new parameters may present themselves and new situations may arise, unforeseen phenomena or occurrences, sometimes in contradiction or without a common link with those that preceded them. Then the initial arrangement has to be modified so that the new reality, the new quality chosen, can be logically incorporated into the edifice. It is therefore reasonable to think that mythical universes reflect, in their form, in their finish, the history of the human groups that have elaborated them.

Thus, certain societies will have had the opportunity to perfect the logic of their constructs and to extend them to new areas; whereas others, often disrupted, will have had to break them up and remodel them over and over again in order to integrate new elements into the existing structure. These differences of historical context are of course compounded by others relating to economic practices, habitation, mentality, and so forth. The Dogon, for example, directed their energies toward merging into a harmonious whole all that had captured their interest, and they even brought all their activities into line with the preestablished model. The mythical structure of the Guajiro, on the contrary, has not been properly finished. And it can be said that, detached from the Arawak groups initially confined to the Amazonian basin, subsequently settling in an area whose physical characteristics differ from those of their original territory, then ill-treated by "History," the Guajiro have never had time to perfect their mythology or have never felt the need to do so. Furthermore, the fact of their living in scattered settlements has surely contributed to the imperfection of a mythology that is transmitted by small groups whose memorizing capacity is obviously reduced and whose interest in exacting intellectual constructs is less pronounced.

Is it perhaps also because of this very imperfection that during several centuries many features of Western society were able to be integrated without difficulty into this relatively loose intellectual universe?

But at present change follows upon change, imposed from outside. The process of transformation is too rapid. Life is disrupted and the myth-making faculty seems to have lost its potential for analysis and stabilization. More than ever, the Guajiro are the prey of History.

Is it not for this reason that we feel doubly concerned by their tales? We the *alijunas*, the foreigners, the non-Guajiros, the non-Indians? The *alijuna*—here an ethnologist—who was the repository of the myths and through whom they will "survive" in our books, the *alijuna* who thought he was alien to this remote world, discovered that he had a place in it. But hardly had he begun to feel an integral part of the Other's universe than he was forced to realize that he was part of the Guajiro death. In personifying *wanülü*, bringer of death, we give him our features. And, placed on the side of death, we truly assume this function: the defenders of a civilization blindly bent on expansion and conquest, we participate today in the destruction of Guajiro civilization. Through their myths, the Guajiro ineluctably recall this "dialectic," as though our dialogue with Others must involve death. As though the Other's death could be related only by us, the harbingers of death.

Notes

1. Or Goajiro (pronounced "Gwa-hi-ro"). This was the name given to the group by the Spanish settlers. The Guajiro refer to themselves by the name of *wayu*.

2. A first partition took place at Bogotá in 1883 (Michelena-Pombo treaty). Challenged by the Venezuelan Congress, it was modified in 1891 after the arbitration of the king of Spain; again in 1923 on the decision of the Swiss federal government, chosen as mediating power; and finally in 1941 (Santos-Lopez treaty). At present the two countries are contesting this last decision.

3. In the case of Venezuelan Guajira, the figures given in the various official bulletins are inconsistent:
   - 22,000 Indians, including 4,000 in Maracaibo, in *Boletín Indigenista Venezolano* (*B.I.V.*), Año VIII (Caracas 1963).
   - 35,000 in *B.I.V.*, Año X (1964–65).
   - "About 14,000" in *B.I.V.*, Año XII–XV (1967).

These fluctuations may be partly accounted for by unverifiable border movements. But the true reason seems to be that no serious or systematic census has ever been taken.

In the case of Colombia, the following information is given:
   - 50,142 [*sic*] in *Diccionario geográfico de la Guajira* (Bogotá, 1944), 120–125. These figures derive from a survey that seems to have been conducted on a systematic basis in 1938. According to the findings, the Guajiro are distributed as follows: Serrania de Jarára: 4,713; Serrania de Cocinas: 3,692; Serrania de Makuira: 3,058; coast and plains: 38,679.
   - 44,748 [*sic*] in Reichel-Dolmatoff (1952). (See Guhl [1963], p. 60).

4. Both the Guajiro names and the scientific names of the animals and plants cited in English in the text are given in the index.

5. In Guajiro this unit is called *michipüle*, or *pichipala*, literally "the place of the houses" (from *michi*, or *pichi*, "house, dwelling").

6. These are, then, in the strict sense, *matrisibs* and not *matriclans*. The Guajiro word designating this entity is *eiruku*, which also means "meat" or "flesh." For instance, *teiruku* means "my clan," "my flesh," or "my meat"; *keiruka* means "to belong to a clan" or "to have some meat."

7. Watson (1967) is the first to have tried to define these units. He distinguishes between *maximal matrilineages* and *minimal matrilineages*. The former are described as localized fragments of matrisibs; the latter are said to be composed of individuals descended by matrilineal filiation from a common ancestor, generally two or three generations distant from a young adult.

Although the *maximal matrilineage* is not a named unit, it seems to be at least indirectly recognized by the Guajiro. It is in fact what is being referred to when, speaking of their "clans," they follow the proper name of the matrisib (Aapüshana, Epieyu, Epinayu, Iipuana, Jayaliyu, Jitnu, Uliana, and so on) by the name of an animal differing from place to place. Thus they speak of the *Uliana-kalaira* (literally, "Uliana-jaguar") who live in the southwest of the Indian zone, of the *Uliana-atpana* ("Uliana-rabbit") who live in the northwest of the peninsula, and of the *Uliana-musa* ("Uliana-cat") in the northeast. Furthermore, new clan names derived from traditional names have emerged. They are applied, according to the Guajiro, to groups geographically detached from the original clans. This is said to be true of the Amapüshana (clan whose "totemic animal" is the horse and whose name is alleged to be a contraction of *ama-Aapüshana*, "horse-*Aapüshana*"), the Sholiyu (branch of the Epieyu clan located around Shoikalu whose totemic animal is the mule), the Waririyu (a branch of the Jitnu clan whose name derives from *walirü*, "fox," the totemic animal of the Jitnu), and others.

If we can believe the authors of the last century, who describe the Guajiro as being organized into clans in the strict sense, this situation is a new one. However, careful scrutiny of the maps drawn up by some of them reveals cause for doubt (see Candelier [1893], Ernst [1887], Reclus [1881], and Simons [1885]). For instance that of Simons, who seems to have been a particularly meticulous observer, shows the same clan names in regions very distant from one another. It should also be stressed that some authors of that period, baffled by the association of several "totemic animals" with a particular clan, endeavored to identify the "true totemic animal," considering that the other animal names merely reflected the ignorance of their informants. This also shows how old the phenomenon is.

According to Watson, a maximal matrilineage is composed of 150–500 individuals and consists on an average of nine minimal matrilineages (a maximum of fifteen, a minimum of five). The name designating the minimal matrilineage could be *apüshi*, "kinship." Based on a principle of filiation, this group is theoretically dispersed. However, it is formed around the nucleus constituted by the matrilocal extended family comprising the nuclear families of the married sisters, their mother, and their children, of the unmarried ones in the case of boys.

Here is not the place to define the function of these units. But, simplifying greatly, it may be said that the maximal matrilineage is the largest political and legal unit of Guajiro society. Its importance depends on the number and wealth of its members and on the prestige of its "chief" (*alaüla*, a word whose primary meanings are "maternal uncle" and "old man"). The minimal matrilineage, whose functions are—on a smaller scale—comparable to those of the maximal matrilineage, is theoretically at the present time the largest exogamous group (in reality, all first- and second-degree relatives are subject to the prohibition against incest, but among third-degree relatives only parallel-matrilateral female cousins are barred from being taken as wives).

8. In most societies polygyny defines an "elite," since under normal demographic conditions it cannot be practiced by everyone. Among the Guajiro it is a sign of wealth and a token of prestige. It usually consists in successive marriages, after each of which several years may elapse. The man generally spends most of his time with his most recent wife, but he does not for all that forsake the previous ones, to whom he pays regular visits. Some Guajiro thus have as many as seven or eight wives. In a sample of two hundred marriages, forty-two were found to be polygynous: five were of the sororal type, twenty-two were with a number of wives ranging from three to five, and only one was with seven wives; all the others corresponded to bigamy.

PART ONE. *SÜKÜJALA ALAÜLAYU:* TALES OF THE ELDERS

1. By the word *a'in,* translated here as "soul," the Guajiro designate the heart as an internal organ and/or as a constituent principle of individual identity. The context does not always make it possible to decide between these two meanings.

2. *Asheyu:* an immaterial being associated with the Guajiro shaman (and sometimes also with the diviner). Under certain conditions—absorption of tobacco juice, shaking of a rattle—the shaman can communicate with that *spirit* who tells him how to effect the cure and assumes responsibility for seeking the sick man's *soul.* A shaman often possesses several *spirits.*

3. Or *wopu wayu ouktüsü,* literally "way Guajiro dead." Another expression used to designate the Milky Way is *spüna yoluja,* "way of the *yolujas,"* or *wopu jepiramüin,* "way to Jepira." It is also, but much more rarely, given the specific name *a'uy* (or *o'uy*).

4. "Rain" is the first meaning of the Guajiro word *juya.*

5. *Tulu:* small, narrow bench made of a single piece of wood, generally zoomorphic, on which the shaman sits when effecting a cure. Today, when they are figurative, *tulus* almost always represent horses or mules. Some Guajiro claim that, in days gone by, *tulus* could take the form of fearsome animals, such as the jaguar or the boa, but this assertion is contested.

6. Guajiro Indians who do not practice stock farming but live exclusively from hunting, food gathering, and horticulture. In the last century there were still many *kusinas,* mainly in a mountain range in the southeast of the peninsula, near Cojoro, known as "the mountain of the *kusinas."* Some Guajiros consider that the *kusinas* (in Spanish: *cosinas*) were "wild and ferocious." Sometimes the name *kusina* is also used by the Guajiro to designate those Indians who are not Guajiro, in contrast with *alijunas,* the whites, and *wayus,* the Guajiro.

7. The everyday dress of a Guajiro man consists of a loincloth (*wusi* or *aiche*) held by a broad belt made of woven wool (*si'ira*), to which are attached pompoms (*si'irapana*) and small crocheted bags (*riula* or *susu*) in which they put tiny objects. The quality and colorfulness of the belt depend on the wearer's social position.

Nowadays, when a Guajiro man moves out of his home territory, he puts on a European-type shirt (*kamisa*, from the Spanish *camisa*) and often wears a hat (*woma*). But the wealthy cover their loincloths with a kind of robe (*nüshein palajana* or *nüsheinpala*). Descending to just above the knee, it consists of a large piece of industrial fabric wound around the hips and kept in place by the belt. In former times the wealthy wore a large woollen cloak (*shewe*) woven by the women.

8. *Oulakawa* or *einawa* (*ainawa*), literally "throwing to one another," designates a ritual game of skill practiced by pairs of men. The object is to be the first to touch one's partner with parts of plants prepared beforehand, such as pieces of torch cactus (*yosü* or *kayuusi*), *yoshushula* (cactaceae), certain creepers (*walerü*), or tuber fragments from the *jourai* (a kind of yucca with white flowers known as the *yucca casanera* in Venezuelan Spanish: *Craniolaria annua*). This game is very often prescribed by shamans at the end of a cure in accordance, so they say, with the wishes of their *spirits*. Sometimes men who happen to be together challenge one another to play the game.

9. *Alijuna* denotes a foreigner, but only when he or she is a white or a non-Indian representative of Western society.

10. Among the Guajiro, ritual weeping (*ayalajakat*) accompanies the whole burial ceremony, whether on the occasion of a first or a second burial. But it is also practiced on exceptional occasions, for instance at the unexpected return of a relative or an ally who has been exposed to great danger or who was presumed dead, as is the case here.

11. Literally, "he who heats up," from *ayaja*, "to heat, to scald with water."

12. *Wüinpümüin* (from *wüin*, "water"): toward the northeast part of the peninsula, the region known as Upper Guajira; in contrast to *wopumüin* (literally, "toward the way"): toward the southern part of the peninsula, the region known as Lower Guajira. The Guajiro distinguish four other main directions (and hence four other regions) in their territory: *jalaala-müin*, "toward Jalaala" (Jalaala is the name of the central, mountainous part of Guajira); *anoulimüin*, "toward the plain" (low-lying northwestern area); *palaamüin* (literally, "toward the sea"), toward the north and northwestern coast; and *jasaleomüin*, "toward the dunes" (southeast coast of the peninsula).

13. This name, derived from *pala*, "sea," is used to designate either the Guajiro living mainly by fishing or the Paraujano Indians. The latter live near Venezuelan Guajira in the lagoon of Sinamaica, where they dwell in houses on stilts. This Arawak group, which is becoming extinct, speak a language very close to that of the Guajiro, from whom some authors believe it to have recently splintered off. Like the Guajiro *parauja*, they live from fishing and horticulture.

14. This is the sign that they are in the presence of a supernatural being. The Guajiro claim that, in the presence of a person embodying a supernatural being, for a short moment one is compelled by a "force" to turn one's gaze away or to lower one's head. This is enough to cause the being in

question to vanish or to change form. In all cases it is a bad omen. Such an encounter is often accompanied by shivering or "tinglings in the body" foretelling sickness or death. In the words of the frightened victim, *kayamülasü tata nütuma*, "I have felt the force . . ."

15. Proper name of this mythical animal. Other storytellers call it Semayui or Kannawüi ("Decorated Serpent").

16. Names of stars and seasons: the Pleiades and probably Hamal (or Sirius).

17. The Guajiro assign considerable economic value to jewels, some of which may, for instance, count as a large part of the bride price paid by the family of the man to the family of the future bride. *Tu'umas* are cut stones made from red jasper or coral and usually set in necklaces. Their value depends mainly on their size and shape. Of lesser value are *kurulashis*, jewels made from red coral and obtained from foreign merchants; *kasuchis*, made of greenish stones; *julujushis* (reddish stone); and *sattas* (light red). A fine *tu'uma* necklace can be worth as much as several dozen head of cattle. Nowadays these jewels are set in metal, often gold or silver, which tends to modify the scale of values.

18. The troopial's pouch-shaped nest can measure almost a yard from top to bottom. It is so finely made that it might be thought to be woven. It generally hangs from a tree and thus suggests the bags known as *susus* that the Guajiro frequently attach to the timberwork of their houses.

19. *Anatashi tashiyuyale pia, majulekalu pioloju alaülayakalu pa'in talaüla tamüle müin. . . . Ashiyu* designates the youngest brother of a woman or a parallel cousin born after her. *Alaüla* designates the mother's brother. But, in a broader sense, this word also describes an aged person, an "elder." And even if it is applied to a young person, the kinship term *alaüla* faintly suggests old age. This accounts for Pulowi's remarks. But immediately establishing an imaginary kinship relation with a stranger is not common among the Guajiro. Here it provides a hint of the hero's particular fate.

20. *Uchi:* this word designates any animal that flies (bird, insect, and so on) or, more generally, any wild animal. But in some contexts it is synonymous with *wanülü*.

21. This refers to the provisional and extremely rudimentary shelter built by the Guajiro who, in the dry season, leave their territory with their herds to settle for awhile in less hard-hit areas (see Photograph 4).

22. In the last thirty or forty years many Guajiros have left Upper Guajira, or the region of Jalaala, to go and settle in the region of Wa'nna. This population movement is partly due to overgrazing and climatic changes, as the Guajiro assert, but it also coincides with the development of a market economy and reflects the desire of a growing number of Indians to draw nearer the boundary between the native territory and the Venezuelan and Colombian national societies. In addition, the newly occupied land is fertile and good for stock breeding.

23. Probably what is involved is a variety of *anolis*, a small saurian reptile of the Iguanidae family.

24. *Awalajia:* "payment." The reference here is to "wergeld," that is, to the compensatory payment that must be made to the victim's group (here the Pulowi matriclan) by the perpetrator of a homicide (Juya).

25. The Guajiro word for menstrual period is *sükashia,* deriving from *kashi,* "moon" or "lunar month."

26. In Guajiro: *sütuma shiira jokoche,* literally "with-this brown-lizard's piss." This is the name derisively given to a short drizzle.

27. The storyteller was not able to recall the name of this bird. But judging by his description, it is certainly a kind of frigate bird (bird of the order Pelecaniformes). No one was able subsequently to give us any further information about Maleiwa's maternal grandfather.

28. According to some Guajiros, this young woman, Maleiwa's future mother, was Siichi, the name of the plant (*Pereskia guamacho*) whose fruit, mixed with that of the plant *manna* (*Tribulus cistoides*), is used to make a type of beer. According to others, she was Manna.

29. *Epeyüi* is the name that is often given by the Guajiro to any supernatural jaguar, that is, one capable of assuming human form. Furthermore, *Kulirapata* is the proper name generally attributed to the primordial jaguar-man that Maleiwa will have to confront. In the story reproduced here, he is designated equally by *kalaira* (jaguar), *epeyüi,* and *Kulirapata.*

30. This is a faithful description of the usual behavior of the Guajiro hunter or fisherman.

31. According to some storytellers, the boys were called Maleiwa, Ulapayüi (or Ulap), and Tümajüle. According to others, Ulap was the name formerly given to Maleiwa. The latter is sometimes nicknamed "Big Belly" (*mülio'u aleechi*). There are also some who claim that Tümajüle was not Maleiwa's brother but his grandmother . . .

32. *Niakai matsayülin a'in chii emüliakai pülashikai:* literally, "he still-without-strength this-one the-youngest the-*pülashi* (the possessor of super-natural powers)."

33. Or *kulira:* animal with a shell (of the *warutta* category), which, when it rains, emits a sound resembling that of a frog. It is supposed to "always contain water" and the Guajiro suck it when they can find nothing else to drink. This animal usually remains stuck to trees.

34. *Jata,* a tree (*Haematoxylon campechianum*) whose bark is marked with deep grooves. From its wood a red dye is obtained.

35. For the Guajiro homosexuality is a sign of feminization but also of animality. There is no more offensive insult for a Guajiro than to be called *asinashi* (pederast).

36. This "saga" was never recounted to me by a single storyteller with the same amount of detail for every episode. Instead, each recorded version develops some episodes but alludes only cursorily to others or even disregards them altogether. As this myth is not the subject of an extensive analysis and is seldom heard, I have reproduced it here in a form that contains the most complete version of each episode, even though this involves distinct changes of style. Each change of storyteller is indicated by the symbol ($\rightleftharpoons$).

37. *Guaimaro* (Spanish; *Byrsonima coriacea?*), a tree that grows in the high areas of Guajira.

38. Some Guajiros claim that she is the daughter of Kulirapata, the jaguar-*epeyüi*; others call her Worunka.

PART TWO. ANALYSIS

I. Guajiro Oral Literature and Structural Analysis

1. Thanks to the kindness of J. Wilbert, who in 1972 opened up to me the card index of the Latin American Center of the University of California at Los Angeles, I have been able to sift through all the documents that have appeared to date concerning the oral literature of the Guajiro. In Table N-1 I indicate the importance and quality of each of them.

TABLE N-1

Author	Date of Publication	Pages	Number of Stories	Quality
Isaacs	1884	206–207	1	R
Hernández de A.	1935	43–44	1	R
Chaves	1946	305–331	15	R
Pineda	1947*a*	114–126	4	R, E (Chaves)
Pineda	1947*b*	37, 76, 145	3	R, E (Chaves)
Caudmont	1953		5	R, G
Chaves	1953	175–176	1	E (Bolinder)
Candelier	1893	270–272	1	R
Gutiérrez de P.	1948	169–171	1	E Bolinder
Izquierdo	1956	293 (8 lines)	1	E (Isaacs)
Bolinder	1957	159–164	6	R
Wilbert	1962	103–104, 112–113	2	R, G
Fuchs	1962	586	1	R
Watson	1968	30	1	E (Fuchs)

R: Reinterpretation; the stories have been told in Spanish, either directly by a bilingual Guajiro or through an interpreter.
E: Tale derived from another author whose name appears in parentheses.
G: Flagrant errors of interpretation marring the document.

Most of these tales concern the Maleiwa cycle and are generally limited to the episodes concerning the origin of humankind.

A book devoted to Guajiro mythology that has recently been published in Venezuela deserves special mention. *Mitos, leyendas y cuentos Goajiros* (Instituto Agrario Nacionale: Caracas, 1973) is the work of Ramón Paz, a bilingual Guajiro. A schoolteacher brought up outside the Indian zone, Ramón Paz returned some years ago to his native culture, in which he is passionately interested. His book is important. It is marked, however, by a pronounced concern with literary form, so that it sometimes seems to stray away from the manner in which the Guajiro tell stories and perhaps from their mythical thought; one cannot help feeling the author's deep-seated desire to display Guajiro oral literature "in the best possible light." But the existence of such men as Ramón Paz, capable of speaking for the Guajiro, eager to do so, and encouraged by the Indians themselves, is a hopeful sign for the future of that civilization.

2. In Guajiro: *jayeechi* or *jayeichi*; "to sing" is *eiraja*.

3. Guajiros claimed that formerly all traditional tales were sung. Nowadays songs with a mythical subject matter are rare.

4. They would, however, be of great interest to anyone wishing to undertake an ethnohistorical study of the Guajiro.

5. The usual term in Guajiro is *shirajain autsü* (feminine) or *nirajain autshi* (masculine), literally "she (he) sings the shaman."

6. Apparently the Guajiro do not have any specific word to designate this genre, apart from the word *kuentshi*, deriving from the Spanish *cuento*. Similarly, they do not refer to a typology of genres of spoken tales, as do other societies. They barely distinguish between "what the elders relate," *süküjala laülayu* or *sükuaitpa wayu alaüla*—traditional stories—and individual anecdotes or forms of expression, *aküjala wane wayu*, "what so-and-so relates."

They generally notify the listeners of the subject to be related by means of circumlocutions signaled by such expressions as *nüchukua* (if the subject is masculine) or *süchukua* (if the subject is feminine), "on the subject of . . . ," or by *nükuaitpa* or *sükuaitpa*, "after the manner of . . ." (from *akuaitpa*, a polysemic word that can be rendered by "mode, manner" or "conduct, procedure" or "custom"). A tale will begin, for instance, with the words *nüchukua wayu jashichi sümaiwa . . .* , "on the subject of a fierce Indian of yesteryear . . . ," or *nükuaitpa Juya*, "after the manner of Juya," unless the tale is simply introduced by such expressions as *taküjeechi wane nükuentshi . . .* , "I am going to tell you the story . . . ," or even more simply by *eshi wane wayu* or *etashi wane wayu*, "there was a Guajiro who . . . ."

7. The questions asked of the Indians—either through interpreters or directly to bilingual Indians—were perhaps slanted by investigators in such a hurry to get to the "essential" that they forced them to speak above all of Maleiwa, the Cultural Hero. But another reason can be found for this distortion. The juxtalinear translation of the Guajiro tales, undertaken very shortly after the first recordings were made, revealed to me that what the bilingual Indians unfailingly translated as "God" ("Dios") or labeled "Maleiwa" could appear in the vernacular text under the name of Juya, Iiwa, or Iruala, as well as Maleiwa, while the words *wanülü*, *pulowi*, *keralia*, and *yoluja* were always rendered as "Devil" ("Diablo") or "Yoluja." This is clearly the result of prolonged contact between Guajiro society and Western society and is due especially to the missionaries. It may be assumed that the latter, immediately on arriving, took pains to find Indian equivalents for the concepts of God, particularly God the Creator, and of the Devil. They easily found the first in Maleiwa, who is depicted in the myths

as fashioning men from clay, and the second in *yoluja*, which is normally an incarnation of a dead person. All the other supernatural beings would then have been brought into line with this simplified dualistic structure. Thus it is not surprising to hear bilingual Indians or converted mestizos constantly alluding to "Maleiwa" or "Yoluja." This also accounts for the silence or reluctance of a large number of Guajiros to talk about them to *alijunas*, since the latter always represent themselves as the only ones with "true" knowledge of those two supernatural beings!

8. Since this book was written I have carried out seven more field studies in Guajira and can confirm this. The two prior investigations (1969–70 and 1973) were conducted in Koushotki (Sierra Jalaala, Colombia, 1973), Makalaitpao (southeast coast, Colombia, 1973), Wüinkua (southeast coast, Venezuela, 1969–70, 1973), Aulejemerai (Sierra Jouitpana, Venezuela, 1969), Pararu (southeast coast, Venezuela, 1969–70, 1973), Karakito (at the foot of the Sierra Wanna, Venezuela, 1973), and Ziruma (suburb of Maracaibo, Venezuela, 1973)—that is, in regions subjected to varying degrees of pressure by Western society, from those regarded as the most isolated and traditionalistic areas to the most acculturated ones (see the map of Guajira at the beginning of this volume).

Paradoxically, it was not in what seemed to be the most isolated regions that I obtained the most telling information. More subject to the phenomenon of rural exodus, they seem to have lost their most active and curious members—the bearers of the "symbolic culture"—drawn to the more wide-open areas or even to the market towns of the border areas (Paraguaipoa, Maicao, Uribia, Riohacha) and the suburbs of Maracaibo.

2. Juya and Pulowi

1. Literally, "hits the rain." *Eitta* or *aitta:* "hit; shoot, throw; fall to the ground"; *-kat* (*-ka* or *-kot*) is the suffixed definite article, denoting the feminine singular; *-sü* is a suffix denoting the third person of the feminine singular in the present tense (in contrast with *-shi*, the same suffix but for a masculine subject).

2. Literally, "it drizzles a rain." *Ememeja* (or *ememaja*): "to drizzle."

3. In order to understand clearly certain aspects of Guajiro mythology it is useful to have a precise idea of the climatic conditions prevailing in Guajiro territory. The climate of the Guajira peninsula is characterized by a system of extremely pronounced seasons. The main rainy season (*juyapu*) runs from September or October to November or December. It is followed by very rapid growth of vegetation and in particular the appearance of "pastures" in many places in the Indian territory. From December or January to April an easterly or northeasterly wind blows, corresponding to a season of drought and relative cold (called *jemiai*). It usually ends in April or May with a slackening of the wind and a few showers, causing the vegetation to start growing again. This is the second rainy season, known as *iiwa*. It gives way to a long dry season, extending from May to September, which is characterized by a steady east wind, increasingly violent and increasingly hot.

In Guajiro it is designated by the words *jouktaleu* (from *jouktai*, the east wind) or *jouktai-jamü*, literally "wind-hunger." But it generally rains very little or not at all in April or May, and this second dry season follows the first without transition. It is usually very severe and sometimes terrible for people and domestic animals, who are then deprived of water and food. The vegetation gradually disappears; the wind carries with it sand and dust. The men set out with their herds in search of the last waterholes and the remaining patches of vegetation.

Figures N-1 and N-2 show the main features of the climate in Guajira.

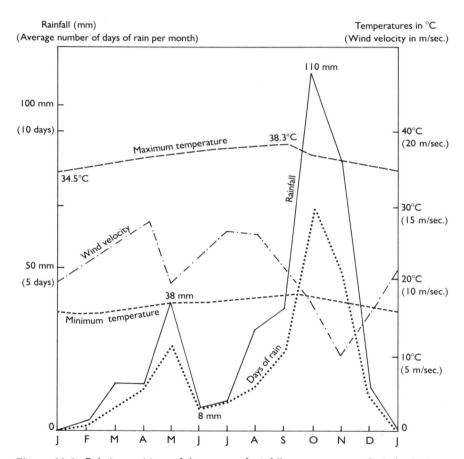

Figure N-1. Relative positions of the curves of rainfall, temperature, and wind velocity. The figures correspond to mean values summarizing meteorological measurements made over a period of ten years (1938–1947) by the Sección de Clima e Investigación Agricola del Ministerio de Agricultura of Colombia. During that period yearly average rainfall was 340 mm (with 25.3 days of rain per year).

4. In the sense of "year," *juya* is used in expressions such as *sülatapa wane juya*, "a year passes," literally "she-passed a year" (from alata, "to pass, to cross," *sü-* denoting the feminine singular); or *kettain juya*, "when the period had elapsed," literally "it suffices years." Used in this sense, *juya* seems to be able to be treated equally as feminine or masculine. *Auyase* appears, for instance, in the expression *nükü̈jain nuyasekat*, "he said his age."

5. Any small and clearly marked opening made in a garment, in the ground, in a wall, etc. For instance, the "perforation of the earlobe" is *so'u ache;* the "door of the house," *so'u michi* or *micho'u;* the "snake's hole," *so'u wüi.*

6. Some people say that all the other rains (*juyakanü:* "the rains") each have their *so'u,* their hole (or their eye), represented by the star that gives them their name. The only difference is that in all such cases the name of the corresponding star is exactly the same as that of the rain; it is no longer marked by the suffix *o'u.* Thus, Iruala signifies at one and the same time the star Spica and the rains that generally usher in the wet season in September.

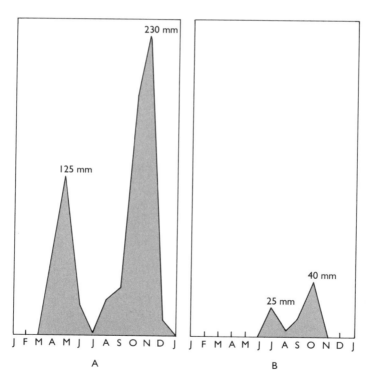

Figure N-2. Examples of extreme years. A: abnormally wet year (1942); B: abnormally dry year (1947).

Pamü (or Ichii) signifies Vega and the rains that announce the end of the wet season. Oümala (Sirius?) denotes the sometimes violent June rains, and Iiwa, the Pleiades, the first rains of the "short wet season." For further details, see the section "Rain and Drought."

7. The "arms of Juya," from *atüna*, "arm, wing, branch." Thus *stüna uchi* means the "wings of a bird"; *stüna wunu'u*, the "branches of a tree." *Katünasü*, literally "it who has wings," is the Guajiro name for airplane.

8. Moreover, this representation is the subject of controversy. Some assert that Juya has only one arm, the northern one, corresponding in reality to the most clearly outlined constellation. To justify this anomaly, those who hold this view refer to an accident: Juya is said to have had an arm torn off by an over-enthusiastic partner in the course of a game of *ka'ulayawa*, the "game of the goat," one of the principal Guajiro festivities (see Chapter 4; Fig. 3).

9. It should be stressed, however, that in the Guajiro language gender is not strictly defined as it is in other languages such as French. The same word with the same meaning may be masculine or feminine. However, the choice of gender sometimes entails the choice of a particular meaning; this is often the case with polysemic words. Thus *wunu* means "tree" when it has a masculine agreement (*wunu'ukai*) and "wood" when it has a feminine one (*wunu'ukat*). Only agreements according to the sex of persons are free from ambiguity. When the object is personified, as is the case here, the gender is strictly defined when the word refers clearly to the personage; thus *Juya* (Rain), *Ka'i* (Sun), and *Kashi* (Moon) are represented by men and treated as masculine. But, especially in the case of *Kashi*, they can be treated either as feminine or as masculine when they refer to the object.

10. Pronounced *püloui*, *pülawi*, *pülowi*, or *pulowi* according to the region and the person speaking. Here the last spelling will always be used, as it is the easiest for us to say; the first, however, corresponds to the most common Guajiro pronunciation.

11. Rising to a height of eight hundred to a thousand meters, these mountains nevertheless seem very high. The Guajiro regard them as *anasü*, "inoffensive," good.

12. This word is written with a capital *P* only when its first meaning is that referred to here.

13. It has become customary for bilingual Guajiros to translate this concept by the Spanish word *encantado*, "enchanted." The word *pulouili* is also used. The expression *puloulira ma* is rendered by "*pulowi* land." The words *pulouli tia makat, nojotsü anairüin* met with in one myth were translated by a bilingual Indian as follows: "this land is always bad; it has not yet become good."

14. This verb is most frequently encountered in the forms *pülashi* or *pülasü*, masculine and feminine, respectively, in the first-, second-, and third-person present. All the Guajiro mythical beings, and particularly Juya and Pulowi, are referred to as *pülashi* or *pülasü*, thus revealing that they all have supernatural, magical powers. But the term is not reserved

exclusively for them. It is commonly attributed to the shaman. One frequently hears the expressions *outshi pülashikai* or *outsü pülasükat*, literally "shaman the-learned" in the masculine and feminine, respectively. They allude to the specific knowledge of the shaman but also to his or her relations with the supernatural world. Sometimes, the words *pülashikai* (m) or *pülasükat* (f) alone, literally "the learned one," are used as synonyms of *outshi* (*outsü*). By extension, anyone whose knowledge is greater than average is termed *pülashi*. *Pülasüinjaya wayukot tia* may be translated by "that woman was very learned" (implying, for instance, that she possessed exceptional knowledge of diseases or of medicinal plants) or by "that Indian woman was dangerous" (implying that she had evil powers). In reality these two meanings coexist, and only the context makes it possible to judge which is being stressed.

Pülasü tamüin sheju ekükat may be translated by "the smell of the food hurts me," implying: it is dangerous for me and hence forbidden. *Pülasü kasa tia* may be rendered by "these things are forbidden (taboo)," *pülasü asika* by "it is forbidden to copulate." Usually these are prohibitions formulated by shamans.

15. "*Sümaiwa pülaiwa makat,*" said one storyteller at the end of a tale, which means literally "in olden times—*pülaiwa*—the earth." One bilingual Guajiro rendered this expression as "before, when all was mixed together on earth, when everything was interchangeable," another as "when the earth was *pülasü*."

16. Such is the case, for instance, in the sentence *ama apülajashi wayu nümüin:* "the horse transformed itself into a Guajiro for him" (literally, "horse transformed-itself into-Guajiro for-him").

17. Or *uchipülainwa*. The victims of these animals "that contaminate" are sometimes described as *pülajüshi*, or *pülajüsü*.

18. A large number of snakes but especially the *sarut* boa; iguanas; a large number of birds including the royal vulture, the urubu, the falcon, the bittern; certain mammals such as the skunk, the squirrel, the tapir, the carcajou; certain fishes including the grouper *malijua* and the *chuchu* are considered by the Guajiro to be very *kapülainsü*. But this list is not restrictive. The fact is that the final diagnosis can be made only by shamans, who in Guajiro society have some scope for innovating. Thus they can always decree that such and such an animal is responsible for the woes of the person consulting them.

The Guajiro also speak of diseases known as *süpülain wayu* (or *nüpülain wayu*). These are said to be caused by "the mere force of the gaze" of certain individuals. This "evil eye" is alleged to be the privilege of those who have killed human beings. "*Nüpülainsü tepichi nirüin,*" one sometimes hears being said of someone: "His gaze is dangerous for small children!"

Another Guajiro disease is called *jipüpülainwa*, literally "to be contaminated by bones." It results from direct contact with the mortuary remains exhumed at the second Guajiro burial (see "Guajiro Burial" section in Chapter 3).

19. All Guajiro girls are required at puberty to undergo a period of seclusion. This is discussed in Chapter 4.

20. These women are also called *kulamia* or *julamia*. One Guajiro even maintained to me that one should say *pülania*, a word deriving directly from *püla*.

21. Often, however, the word *wanülü* is used as a generic term; it then includes both these meanings.

The sickness known as *wanülü* is often regarded as something that enters a person and must be eliminated by the shaman by means of exorcism. *Ajuitüsü wanülü tatuma*, she will say at the end of the cure: "through my intervention the sickness has gone out." *Shejetüin wanülükat*, "she has spat out the sickness," will then be the comment of those observing the cure.

22. Literally: "to have the wound" (from *alia*, "wound, object that wounds, metal arrow head") or "to have met" (from *ousta*, or *oushta*, "to meet").

23. Also referred to as *aseyu* and *ajuna*. In reality these words are never found in this form but are always preceded by a radical denoting the gender and the person. Thus the shaman will say *tasheyu* or *tajuna*, "my spirit." The observer will speak of *nüsheyu, najuna*, or *süseyu, sajuna*, "his (her) spirit," according to whether the shaman is a man or a woman. The form *washeyu* or *wajuna*, "our spirit," is also very commonly used by shamans.

The radical *ajuna* or *ojuna* is taken from the verb *ajuna:* "to be on or with someone, to accompany, to follow in order to help." Used to qualify the word *aseyu*, it may also be synonymous with it.

24. *Kasheyukot* (or *kasheyukai*), literally "she (he) who has a *spirit*," is synonymous, moreover, with shaman (*autsü, autshi,* or *piachi*). Each shaman possesses at least one *spirit* but on average he or she has three or four.

25. Relating a case history, an old shaman said one day: "*nütkaka wanülükai, esü tü wanülükat nümaka taya wanülü chaya*," which may be translated: "an arrow was shot into him by the *wanülü*, that is his sickness, my spirit over there told me so." Here the word *wanülü* takes on successively all three meanings discussed above.

26. It is doubtless not by chance that it is the shamans, who are the most "knowledgeable" and the best acquainted with the symbolic universe, who speak more readily of *wanülü* than of *tasheyu* or *tajuna* when referring to their *spirit*. For from their standpoint the three meanings here dealt with separately converge. Indeed, it is during sickness (*wanülükat*) that every Guajiro shaman becomes aware of his calling and receives his *spirits* (*wanülükanü*), and it is thanks to the latter that he can recognize and to some extent thwart the *wanülüs*, the beings who bring death.

As I shall show in a future book, this polysemia reflects the particular position of the shaman in Guajiro society and thought. Furthermore, it becomes logical when considered in relation to the Guajiro interpretation of sickness and death. The Guajiro attribute to *wanülü* an almost immediate power of death; this means that he is capable of carrying away the *soul* of the person he has pierced with his arrow in the universe of *Dream*, that "transit zone" which precedes death when there is no return (see Part One, lines 1–73). Shamans also have access to this zone, through their *spirit*. According to this Guajiro theory, then, *wanülü* and the shaman's *spirit* have at least one itinerary in common, since both go from the human world to that in which the *soul* is momentarily a "prisoner."

27. Even more precisely: one shaman told me, boasting of one of his *spirits*, "*wanülü anashana tajuna sümünaka*," which was translated by a bilingual Indian as "they said that my *ajuna* was an excellent *wanülü*," that is, "the *spirit* who protects me is excellent." Another added, to make it clear that he was speaking of his *spirit* and not of the *wanülü* who shoots arrows: "*chi wanülü taseyukai nojoishi moluin, ipünashi, nojotsü sainjayain amüin*," literally "this *wanülü* who-is-my-*spirit* is-not on-the-ground, he-is-on-high, he kills no one."

28. Further proof of this hypermasculinity attributed to Juya can be found elsewhere. In certain tales constituting true variants of the myth "A Secluded Girl Abducted by Juya" (Part One, lines 9022–10,007), the mythical hero is replaced in his role as irresistible seducer by Epeyüi. Epeyüi is a "supernatural jaguar" (*kalaira pülashi*) capable of assuming human appearance (some Guajiros describe him, in his animal form, as a "jaguar without a tail"). For the Guajiro, Jaguar, and a fortiori Epeyüi, is considered to be essentially virile, physically very strong, and a trained fighter, qualities highly valued by the Guajiro man, who may reveal them in public on the occasion of the festival known as *ka'ulayawa*, during which "wrestling bouts" are organized (called *atsüinjirawa* or *atchinjirawa*, from *atsüin* or *atchüin*, "strength," or *apajirawa*, "to clasp oneself"). One myth not cited here tells how, in his human form, Epeyüi succeeds on that occasion in easily defeating the Guajiro reputed to be the most invincible (before dragging him far away from the onlookers and killing him).

If there were need for further proof of the force attributed to the jaguar by the Guajiro, it would be found in the early episodes of the long epic myth recounting the origin and first days of humankind, in which Maleiwa, the Guajiro Cultural Hero, is seen engaged in a running fight with Kulirapata, the human jaguar, at the end of which Maleiwa, of course, has the advantage but not without difficulty (lines 10,198–10,319).

29. That female sex organ which, according to one myth, was originally armed with teeth and wrought destruction among men (lines 10,404–10,410).

30. Thus the Guajiro say that Juya "stays each year for very short periods with two of his wives" in the locality of Juyapia, or Nepia Juya, the "House of Juya." Juyapia is the name given to a deep gully into which torrents of water stream on days of heavy storms. It lies about a mile away from the sea on the northern shore of the bay of Neimalu (Puerto Lopez in Spanish). A few hundred yards from there are two *pulowi* places, Kalinapia and Palasanain: "it is there that his wives live."

31. The Guajiro often refer to places that according to the elders were

formerly *pulowi* but are no longer so today. In almost all cases these "extinct" *pulowis* (now *anasü*, "good") are near areas that were previously lived in but are now deserted or scarcely inhabited (often as a result of extensive population movements over the last few decades toward the border areas and the urban shantytowns).

32. *Sulu'u ma* (or *suupüna molu'u*) and *shiroku pala*, respectively.

33. *Ekerochi yala sakamüin ti so'ukot yala Ayajuli, ekerochi süseromüin makat*, literally "he-penetrates here right-inside this hole here of-Ayajui, he-penetrates right-to-his-middle the-earth."

34. *Shimiralüin püloi, shiküin ma:* "Pulowi has swallowed him, Earth has eaten him," the Guajiro will say for instance about a man who has gone missing.

35. There is, however, an exception to this rule of localization: when, for the purposes of the tale, Pulowi lives close to Juya's abode (cf. "The Journey to the Beyond").

36. It is situated on the eastern coast of Guajira, near Wüinkua.

37. This *pulowi* lies near the Colombian-Venezuelan border, a few miles west of Wüinkua.

38. *Apülajasü süpüla püloui*, literally "she-is-transformed for-her *pulowi*."

39. *Wane wüi müloushana*, "a gigantic snake." *Sarulu* (or *sarut*) designates the boa constrictor, *kasiwanau* a smaller species of boa. Of a whitish color with darker spots, the latter is extremely common in Guajira.

40. The Guajiro word *wüi*, translated here as "reptiles," designates either a category comprising mainly the ophidians and the saurians, or solely the ophidians. In all cases the crocodilians and the chelonians are excluded.

41. *Papüshawasü*, from *apüshi*, "matrilinear kinsman; part of a group."

42. Master of animals or "animal" himself, since the word *uchi* is sometimes taken to be synonymous with *wanülü* (Part One, n. 23). It will be seen later that there is no contradiction here.

43. The Guajiro place them in the category *she'e ma*, "the parasites, the products of the earth." This category also includes animals. Some Guajiro say *sükorolo ma*, "the jewels of the earth," or *shira ma*, "the secretions of the earth."

44. Some Guajiros assert that these famous *josüs* were simply anteaters or great anteaters to which "ignoramuses" transposed the characteristics of the *akalapuis*. It is indeed noteworthy that these two animals, living solely on the southern edge of the Indian zone, are called *oso* (bear) in Venezuelan Spanish (from which the Guajiro name *josü* might derive). In any case, those who believe in them associate them with Pulowi.

45. *Müshichije wayuin chi, niajaya chi makat:* "he resembles a Guajiro, but he is the earth."

46. In Guajiro, the verb *kepeyüla*, clearly from the same root as the word *epeyüi*, is translated by bilingual Indians by such periphrases as "there is something dangerous, like a *wanülü* or a *pulowi*." In its most common forms—*kepeyülüin* or *kepeyüsü* (third-person singular)—this word is, then, almost synonymous with *pülaiwa* or *pulouli*. For instance, it will be

said equally of a particular place: *kepeyülüinja tü* or *pülainjü tü*. The idea thus expressed is that it is unhealthy, as it is probably the dwelling-place of dangerous supernatural beings. This may be seen as further proof of the relationship between Pulowi and Epeyüi.

47. To this list of supernatural beings associated with Pulowi one is tempted to add the very popular figure known as *chama*. In certain versions of traditional tales the place of Pulowi is taken by that "old woman with very long hair who lives in the thickest part of the bush." Most of the Guajiro assert that she attacks only lost children, whom she attempts to devour after she has fattened them. But others regard her as a true personification of Pulowi. In point of fact, this is undoubtedly a new theme, perhaps derived from Venezuelan and European folklore; among the Kuna an identical figure bears the name of Xama. But the only fact of importance here is the existence of a relationship between Chama and Pulowi.

48. I should emphasize that Pulowi does not synthesize all forms of sickness (and death). This is not the place to cite all the Indian concepts bound up with medicine and shamanism, but it may usefully be noted that alongside diseases associated more or less closely with the concepts of *pulowi* and *wanülü*—and among them may be included diseases of the *apülainwa/ kapulainwa* type mentioned above—there exists a category of serious diseases that are not attributed *immediately* to them. These are diseases that are clearly defined clinically and individually named, and hence scientifically identifiable by shamans and also by any thoughtful observer. The Guajiro recognize explicitly that they can bring death, but having means of protection against them—they usually use therapeutic substances derived from plants—they always hope to ward it off. This applies, for instance, to the diseases called *polona* (malaria and other tropical fevers), *yokoroi* (certain eruptive fevers), *shunüi* (designating bronchitis and certain symptoms of tuberculosis), and others.

But if the sickness takes a sudden turn for the worse, there is very often a discontinuity in the diagnosis. A practical explanation is followed by a supernatural one. For instance, the shaman will say of a recognized tubercular patient (*kamusoina ayuishi*, literally "tuberculosis he-is-sick") that he has been pierced by a *wanülü*'s arrow (*nütküin nia wanülü*, literally "he-has-shot that-one *wanülü*") when he becomes afflicted with a clear-cut case of haemoptysis resulting in death. In practice, then, there is always a tendency to give death a religious interpretation, and this is expressed with the help of the concepts of *pulowi* and *wanülü*.

49. *Uchi unapajat kamülüin pulowi, irama kamülüin pulowi*, literally "the-animals of-the-bush she-has-for-domestic-animals *pulowi*, the-deer she-has-for-cattle *pulowi*."

50. Pulowi is sometimes referred to as *süpayalainkat irama*, literally "the deer charmer." However, some Guajiros distinguish between Pulowi and this figure, who is described in one myth as a "sweet and beautiful girl" who, pursued and captured by a hunter, becomes his wife after he has tamed her and accustomed her to human food.

51. Or *jokoliwa*. When, in the mythical tales, this animal is personified, he also appears under the name of Wapata, Wopata, or Joupata. Only the male has a pouch. Flat when at rest, it swells by muscular contraction when the animal is excited. This movement serves apparently to attract the female.

52. *Apayala süpüla juya*, say the Guajiro: literally, "they are effective for the rain." In other words, they are the premonitory signs of rain.

53. *Shiitapa Juya, apünajünajat*, literally "when *juya* falls one must sow." This is a Guajiro saying.

54. The life cycle of the plants cultivated by the Guajiro—ecologically adapted to the semidesert climate—is extremely short; it is completed in a few weeks (three to seven). In addition, the Guajiro reduce the period of dormancy of the seeds by immersing them in water for some ten hours before sowing them at the beginning of the rainy season (this causes the disappearance of the water-soluble growth-inhibitors contained in the seed coats, which can otherwise be washed out only by very abundant rainfall).

55. In Guajiro: *wunu'u*. Depending on its context, this word may mean, "uncultivated plant," "medicine," or "wood" (as material).

56. Some storytellers, however, say that in Pulowi's domain every kind of food abounds, animal or vegetable, cultivated or wild. In this case, they are merely anxious to show that the supernatural world, in contrast with the terrestrial world, is a place where one always eats well.

57. *Müsüka saamatuitkai tü makat anain, nojoluin kasa sulu*, literally "it seems—the cold-this-tranquil-land, there is nothing-inside." In Guajiro, *saamata* means "to be cold."

58. *Kerotsü na'in sulumüin piyushi*, literally "she penetrates his soul into the darkness."

59. *Nojotsü kamawalüin tü wayukoleiru nütuma atamatai piyuwaya ouktüsü:* "The Guajiro who get up at night are not slow in dying because of him (*wanülü*)"; this is said in the way of a proverb (literally: "they-do-not-last those Guajiros because-of-him who-get-up when-it-is-dark they-die").

60. This heavy immobility is called *maychi* or *maitüsü*.

61. *Nia antirakaja juyakai süma, kanierüin shia*, literally "him he succeeds-the-Juya with-her, for-wife-he-has-her."

3. The Journey to the Beyond

1. *Oyolojo* and *ajuya*, respectively. (In Guajiro "shadow" is *jemioushi*—from *jemiai*, "cold, freshness"—when it is given by a tree or any other object affording protection from the heat of the sun.)

2. *Epa süntüin tü yolujaka sünain tü ouktüsü*, literally "there she-arrives this-*yoluja* to that dead-one."

3. *Tü nierüinkat maima echülü*, literally "this-one his-wife many husbands."

4. If a woman is deemed to be guilty of adultery, her husband, supported by his matrilineage, demands substantial economic compensation from his wife's lineage. If it is refused, the dispute may be exacerbated by a blood vengeance.

5. *Alatain, mashulasa, palaatasü nia* ("flesh" is rendered here by *ashula*, "pulp, flesh," and not by *eiruku*, "meat, flesh, clan").

6. In the versions at my disposal, the carrier is either "a Guajiro on horseback," or an *alijuna*, or a "big red ant," *jeyu ishosü*. See also Paz (1973: 93–115).

7. *Chirinchi* (Colombian Spanish): a very strong alcoholic drink—also called *yootsü*, from *yooli*, "little"—generally made from sugar cane. Bought from *alijunas*, it has practically replaced all the different kinds of beer (*shiruna*, made from corn, watermelon, wild fruits, and so on) that were traditionally made by the Guajiro. It has led many Indians into alcoholism, that scourge which in some regions is causing serious social problems.

8. Muskmelon, along with watermelon, is the vegetable food most highly appreciated by the Guajiro. At once a food and a drink, it is easily transportable and keeps for a long time. Great care goes into its cultivation. In addition, its fragrance and taste are always being praised, and for that reason it symbolizes gastronomic pleasure.

9. A dead man's body belongs to his matrilineage. The hero of this tale has consequently committed a serious offense in destroying it. For his part, he is convinced that his wife has committed adultery. This is enough to justify the death of one of her kinsmen: the Guajiro are prone to violence and it is fairly common for their thirst for immediate vengeance to lead them to homicide. A kind of vendetta may then be triggered unless, in the meantime, a *ma'ünai* or *purchipü*, "a man of the word"—a mediator—has been able to settle the dispute by persuading one of the parties to give material compensations (*awalaja nujüniala*, "to pay one's debt") and the other to accept them. We have already seen a similar situation: because his wife Pulowi was unfaithful to him with Iiwa, Juya killed her brother (Part One, lines 8072–8074).

10. The Guajiro verb *amuloule*, "to get lost," expresses the idea of "to lose one's way" but also that of "to lose one's present form, to change state." On occasion it can also be rendered by "to seek misfortune, to court disaster, to go to a certain death" in the sense of acting in an almost suicidal way so as to be likely to have an ill-fated encounter, especially with supernatural beings. It is then almost synonymous with the verb *ayülaja*, "to be disgusted."

11. This is not always true. But in Guajiro *jepirechi* (or *jepirachi*, words deriving from *Jepira*) designates the direction southwest-northeast or a rain-carrying wind blowing in that direction. It is also the "middle direction" of the Milky Way, the "way of the dead Guajiro."

12. *Ounashi taya*, from *ounuawa* or *aunuwawa*: to ask for a material contribution. When, following a serious dispute (murder, wounds, and so on) a Guajiro has to pay substantial damage to people of a lineage other than his own, he usually takes a collection among members of his own lineage to bring together the cattle, objects, and nowadays money demanded by the opposing party.

13. *Presashi taya . . .* : from the Spanish *preso*, "prisoner." No form of

punitive imprisonment is practiced by the Guajiro, but the Indians are generally very impressed by this Western custom that they have all heard about and to which some have been subjected.

14. *Yolujalepa ma'i wanülüin; mapakalia, nojotsü malualüin:* literally, "he-is-*yoluja* enormously into-*wanülü;* much-later, not at-once."

15. *Tü yolujakat yolujasia ne, wanülüsü joo mapaya chi alijunakai süpüla wayu:* literally, "this *yoluja* she-is-*yoluja,* she-is-*wanülü* then much-later this the-*alijuna* toward Guajiro."

16. At this point one is bound to raise the question: What becomes of the *soul* of the Guajiro and where does it come from? For most of the Guajiro the *soul* is a constituent part of the human being and is formed at the same time as the body. Going further back, to the origin of beings, some claim that Kashi, Moon, is "our father" (*kachonjawaya weikat nütüma kashikai, shiirukuwaya tü weikat:* "we-are-the-children-of our-mother with-the-help of-Moon, we are our mother's flesh") (cf. lines 9009–9012, 10,009) and that he is "the one who gives each individual his or her *soul.*" (Kashi might be thought to give life to human beings, since, in causing women to menstruate, he enables them to feed the fetus with their blood—for they cease to menstruate during pregnancy—and since he endows them with a *soul,* while the main function of Juya, who is also the "father of the Guajiro," is to preserve that life.)

This connection between *soul* and Moon is confirmed by certain shamans who say that Moon helps their *spirits* to find the *soul* of the sick in the complete darkness (*piyushi*) in which it moves:

The darkness where we are going never departs
as does the darkness that comes here, on earth . . .
Over there Moon helps our *spirits.*
"It is good that you are working thus!
That's the purpose for which you were made,
that's the purpose for which she was made a shaman,"
says Moon to our *spirits,*
and our *spirits* tell us.

(Words spoken by the female shaman Reachon Aapshana and recorded on September 10, 1973. This shaman, aged about eighty, lives near Piruachon, in Venezuelan Guajira.)

But what happens to *souls* on the "death" of *yolujas?* Are they to be found "in" the rain or "in" *wanülüs?* To these direct questions no traditional answer is ever given. Many Indians think it enough to say that "the *soul* gets lost," *amüloisü sa'inkat.* For others, however, "it is impossible for the *soul* to vanish since in dreams everything is possible; one can meet anybody, any time." In fact this answer is an indirect criticism of the common idea that in dreams one meets only "beings possessed of an identity." And these, as we have just seen, are still *yolujas* and as such are provided with a *soul.* There are also Guajiros who propose solutions that can be disregarded here on account of their being clearly too individualistic and usually confused.

17. *Eiajiraskanü wanülüsü chaya emüinre cha kayatüin, kajüle ouktüs-kolu sütüma wanülü chaya, wanesa maka:* literally, "the-poisoned-ones in-*wanülüs* over-there where-they-go, over-there they-stay-the-same, those who-are-dead by *wanülü* there, thus it-is-said."

18. The division between "the good" and "the wicked" that was suggested by one Guajiro, with reference to the life of human beings on earth, is probably marked by the influence of the Christian West: "There are people who are changed into rains, others into *wanülüs*. The *wanülüs* are the *souls* of the most wicked dead." Perhaps this is also true of the far more frequent assertion that "there are many people beneath (the surface of the earth), as there are above" (*esü wayu wattasalia sopüna, müsiaka chaya ipüna, siru-matü*)—unless this image is regarded as an example of the unconscious use of one of the homological relations highlighted above:

juya : *wanülü* :: high : low.

19. In Guajiro this coffin is called *unna* (from the Spanish *urna*, "coffin"). When it is made by Indians it consists preferably of two hollowed-out halves of the *patsua* tree; this tree (*Erythrina corolladendron?*) is said to have the property of secreting an abundant resin that prevents foul smells from escaping by hermetically sealing the two parts. If not, when the wake is to last a long time, the corpse is periodically removed from the coffin, smeared with alcohol or perfume, rubbed with oil, covered in talcum powder, and nowadays sometimes even injected with formol in order to prevent the atmosphere from becoming so unbreathable that the women no longer find it possible to weep.

According to old Guajiros, the dead person's body used to be folded over on itself, the knees against the abdomen and the hands placed on the front side of the thighs, almost in the fetal position. It was then wrapped in newly skinned cowhide, which was later sewn up.

20. This transfer operation is designated by the verb *aika* or *eika*, which also means "to guide, to show." The place where the dead are buried is called *ojoitüle* (from *ojoita*) or *eiküle* (from *eika*). The departure of the deceased is marked by the shooting of large numbers of arrows or the firing of a salvo toward the sky. According to some, the purpose of this is to keep away from this dwelling-place the *yolujas* "drawn by the corpse."

21. The grave (*amuuyu* or *amouyu*) where the body is laid was in earlier times a short distance away from the house of the deceased, usually on a hill. Nowadays the coffins are very often placed in stone and cement vaults painted white (called *wowira*, from the Spanish *boveda*), copied from the Venezuelan and Colombian model. Set on high ground, the Guajiro "cemeteries," called *sementeria* (from the Spanish *cementerio*) contain several vaults of this type.

Like the ancient tombs, open at ground level, these vaults are nearly always placed in an east-west direction, with variations not exceeding about fifteen degrees on either side of that position. I found only two exceptions to this rule in some fifty "cemeteries" observed, and these were in cemeteries situated in a frontier zone. The opening of the vault is generally on the east side.

A large number of the Guajiro I questioned declared that they were unaware of this regularity. The others offered two explanations to justify this practice. Some claimed that the purpose was to prevent foul odors from disturbing the weeping women assembled near the opening or those who would be coming to disinter the corpse for the second burial. In fact, a strong wind blows from east to west across Guajira for nine to ten months a year. But, while this practical explanation may be convincing when the body is placed in a vault, it ceases to work in the case of traditional burials in graves accessible on all sides. Others considered it essential for the body to lie in this direction because, being parallel to the path of the sun, the dead person—lying on the back, head toward the east—is thereby able to "see the sun go down in the west; and the west is an end, that of the sun's diurnal course, as death is the end of our sojourn on earth."

Some claim that the corpse's head may also be on the west side and justify this by the fact that the moon "may disappear in the east." "We leave with our heads toward the east because of the sun and with our heads toward the west because of the moon," say some, more conciliatory in their attitude.

Thus may be summed up all the information I was able to obtain on the matter. So far, analysis provides no further solution to this problem.

22. Gutierrez de Pineda (1948:159) speaks of a "purification rite" without giving any other particulars. Perhaps she is alluding to the custom of the "family bath" (*o'ojokira* or *shkira o'ojo*, from *o'oja*, "to bathe, to wash oneself") that closed the ceremony of the first burial and at the end of which the matrilinear kin close to the deceased—who had no choice but to undergo it—could share their food with anybody, which they were not allowed to do during the wake. The grave-digger and all the handlers of the corpse generally belong to this group. The bath was taken at nighttime or at dawn, "at the height of the cold" (*jemiai palasü*). Its purpose was to prevent "those close to the clan from dying," for "the clan is like a tree that has to be watered," as I was told by an old Guajiro. Nowadays this rite is very seldom practiced.

23. *Aisü nünülia wane ouktüin, chuntanale nümannaja amüire, süwalajüin:* "It hurts to say a dead person's name. If you do, you have to pay for it," say the Guajiro.

24. *Akochujünüsü shipüshika:* literally, "she-gathers-together the-bones."

25. *Jipupula,* literally "the place of the bones," from *jipu,* "bone." According to Polanco (1958a), the relatives responsible for the exhumation sometimes take the remains to their home where they bury them provisionally (*oupunawa*) or hang them by means of a woven net from the roof frame (*kacheta*) until the day fixed for the second burial.

26. This second-burial vault is often built alongside the larger vaults reserved for the first burial. Like the latter, it is generally half in the earth and half above it and painted white (it is then called *rosaria,* from the Spanish *osario,* more readily than *jipupala*). But, unlike the large vaults in

which various kinfolk or even neighbors can intermingle, it can in theory receive only kin belonging to the same matrilineage (or matriclan). Hence the place of the first burial and that of the second do not always coincide.

27. In order to comply with the logic of their symbolism, have the Guajiro here had to fly in the face of fact? Medically speaking, there is no way of deciding in the absence of prior analysis which is the more virulent, the body of someone who has recently died or a corpse dug up a few years after death, regardless of its state of decomposition. For, although the corpse develops a pathogenic character solely during the two to four days following death, so-called encapsulated forms of certain virulent germs may appear that attach themselves to the corpse, may be preserved for an extremely long time, and survive on the most minute remains or on bones apparently free of decomposed matter. These encapsulated forms develop at the time of exhumation, when the ambient conditions are modified. Some can be extremely pathogenic. In order, then, to answer the question, it would be necessary to make a systematic analysis of the remains exhumed for second burial.

Moreover, it should be stressed that the insalubrity connected with the putrefaction of the body is well known to the Guajiro. It is expressed by the idea of *marüla*. *Marülas* are "beings living on ground"—*marüla molu'uko*—to which, in the words of a shaman, "the *wanülüs* give up the body of him they have just killed." They are also called *yoluja kejüsü,* "foul-smelling *yolujas.*" *Marülas* come out of, and so to speak emanate from, places where the dead are buried. Most Guajiros imagine them to be like *yolujas* (cf. line 54), of which they may be said to be the counterpart since, on the one hand, the *a'in,* the *soul* of the deceased, is "embodied" in the *yoluja,* and, on the other, the body—*atapa,* or *eiruku,* "the skin, the flesh"—puts forth *marülas.*

Like the *yolujas, marülas* are unpleasant rather than really dangerous. However, the shamans consider them to be "capable of evil"—*mojusü, ka'injarakaleirua*—and hold them responsible for certain diseases. Hence the Guajiro prefer to make a detour when they smell their scent or take steps to make them go away. A curious practice engaged in for this purpose was brought to my attention: as soon as the *marüla's* odor enters a house, the eldest son (*eirumakai*) of the family must take out his penis and wave it in the direction of the smell. The *marüla* will then go away, together with the effluvia accompanying it.

28. It will be remembered that the Guajiro depict the *yolujas* as "persons whose bones have been removed." Here the storyteller has interpreted this expression literally.

29. See Perrin (1970: 15–17).

30. According to a free interpretation of this myth recently published by Ramón Paz (1973: 101), the bench turns out to be a peccary: "But how great was the surprise of Ulepala to find that when he sat down on the bench it turned into a huge and furious peccary. The young man, surprised by this untoward occurrence, at once got off the peccary's back. Juya laughed. . . .

He played with the animal."

For the Guajiro the peccary (*piichi*) is one of the most dangerous game animals and one of the most difficult to hunt. This is because it lives in particularly remote and inhospitable areas of Guajira and also because it may turn against its pursuers when wounded. A peccary hunt therefore calls for highly virile qualities. By demonstrating his power over the peccary, then, Juya demonstrates his "hypermasculinity" and also his power over Pulowi, the mistress of game animals.

31. If it were necessary to furnish further proof of the rain being represented by Calabash or Spider, it would be found in the myth "The Pulowi of Ayajui" (lines 534–657). The formal similarity between this tale and the third part of "The Journey to the Beyond" is striking. In the one, a man who has left Jepira because his wife engages in debauchery stays in Juya's domain. There he is killed by Pulowi, then brought back to life by Juya before being escorted back to earth by Calabash or Spider. In the other, two girls suffering from the asocial behavior of their neighbors (or their brothers, Dragonfly and Brown Lizard, in another version) decide to leave "their lands." They are swallowed up by Pulowi, saved then welcomed by Juya, their father, before coming back to earth in the form of rains. This metamorphosis into rain has the same position in this tale as the episode of the descent to earth with Spider or Calabash in "The Journey to the Beyond." This parallel bears out the connection referred to between the rain and one or other of the "carriers."

32. Comparing the different variants of this episode, one might be tempted to give another reason for the choice of these singular carriers, complementary to the previous interpretation. It is to be noted, on the one hand, that the spider and the calabash are by their nature mediators, a fact that has not escaped the notice of the Guajiro. For in the Guajiro mind, the spider, being both a spinner and a hunter, is at the same time associated with woman and man; while the calabash clearly belongs with dryness as regards its specific nature and the way it is made (it is "hard and dry"— *chepan* and *osopan*—say the Guajiro) and with the rain as regards what it contains. It is to be stressed, on the other hand, that in every case this carrier is depicted in the guise of an old woman, whether it is the spider, the calabash, or an unspecified thing: in other words, someone who, in Guajiro society, often enjoys within her lineage powers comparable to those of men (sharing with them the title of *alaüla*, "elder" or "chief"). Thus the character of mediator attributed to the carrier is reinforced. Is this to suggest the destiny awaiting the dead Guajiro? Is this to emphasize the ambiguity of this figure who, for reasons seldom made clear (except in the case of Calabash), saves the hero all the better to bring about his downfall by asking him to respect a humanly untenable prohibition? Nothing points to any definitive answer here.

4. Sükuaitpa Wayu Alaüla: The Custom of the Old Guajiros

1. I have defined the position of a star as the point of intersection of the meridian on which it is situated on a map of the heavens with the line representing the celestial equator. Moreover, this is in keeping with the conception of the Guajiro, for whom all stars situated on the same north-south line "walk" in the same movement and are considered to be equally advanced (it should not be forgotten that Guajira is close to the terrestrial equator). On the other hand, the positions of the other seasons are defined in relative terms, by the Guajiro themselves.

2. The detailed findings of my first study of Guajiro astronomy are set out in Perrin (1973: 417–18).

3. The Guajiro make use of two main types of facial painting. The linear paintings mentioned here are used on the occasion of festivities, chiefly for the *yonna* dance. Originating from plants, they are brick red or dark blue in color, depending on the plants that go to make them up, the *paliisa* (roucou) and the *wanapai* (genipa?: *jaba* or *tapara* in local Spanish), respectively.

Reserved for women and very commonly used, the other facial paintings are spread uniformly over the entire face or that part of it beneath the forehead. The curve that delimits this monochrome surface, symmetrical in relation to the axis of the face, differs from one woman to another (see the Photographs 8 and 11). I noted several dozen types. To this diversity of forms is added a diversity of colors. Three basic colors are used, which give their name to the painting and to the design: black, *mashuka* or *pai'pai;* very dark brown or yellow, *machepü;* and brick red, *paliisa,* more rarely used here. The first three colors are made from mushroom spores. But these colors can be mixed to give an infinite number of intermediate shades. The women claim that the sole function of this painting is to decorate them and, above all, to protect them from the heat of the sun. There does not seem to be any link now between the choice of colors and design and the social identity of the wearer.

4. I might mention, as further proof, that one Guajiro encountered for the first time and hence not influenced by my particular concerns spontaneously said on seeing me try on one of these headdresses, *"müshikanai Juya sulu karatsükat"*: "You look like Juya with that *karatsü.*"

5. A comparable occurrence is related by Pineda (1947). But more than a genuine rite, what is involved is a type of prescription that each shaman adapts with a fair measure of freedom to each particular case. This practice might be described as, so to speak, an individualized rite.

6. *Süttüsü paülü,* literally "she is locked in the house." *Shükonolüsü* derives from *shükona.* The term *paülüasü* is also used, from *paülüwa,* "to be inside the dwelling."

The secluded girl is sometimes referred to as *paülükat,* "she who is in the house," or *majayülü paülü,* "the girl in the house" (from *paü,* "dwelling house"). She is also designated as *süttüsükat,* "she who is locked in."

7. This is referred to as the "piercing," *sojototüin jimo'olu*, literally "she is pierced the girl." "Moon is the first to penetrate and hollow out the woman" (*nüwayushijüin kashi; nojotorüin kashi sümünüin tüü; wayukat majayütüinka;* literally "she is Moon's woman; Moon pierces the girl and makes her a young woman"). The Guajiro also say by way of a dictum: "the little girl becomes a young woman; Moon makes her a young woman" (*eka tepichi majaÿlüin; majayütüsü nütüma kashi münüsü*). Furthermore, menstruation is called *akashia* (or *sükashia*), a word deriving from *kashi*, moon.

8. This voluntary prolongation of the period of seclusion might be the consequence of a custom said to be highly developed "in the olden days": rich families are believed to have wanted certain girls to undergo prolonged seclusion and to have locked them up from their earliest years in order, so it seems, to increase their prestige so that they "might better eat rich men," said by way of a dictum, thus stressing this connection with Pulowi, the "eater of men" (*shimiralüin wayukaluiru*). But there are also young men considered to be *pülainchi* (masculine form of *pülainrü*, a word that the bilingual Guajiro translate as "pretentious, bumptious").

9. As Métraux did when he commented on the predominance of women in Auraucarian shamanism (see Métraux, 1949: 589).

10. A linear sign, often obviously derived from old Spanish cattle-brand marks, is associated with each Guajiro clan. It is reproduced on irons (*jeerü*, from the Spanish *hierro*, "iron") with which cattle or any items of moveable property are branded. Each matrilineage can possess a particular sign, derived from the general mark of the clan it belongs to.

11. See Part One, lines 9009–9013. The "metaphor of the egg," first referred to by Gutierrez de Pineda (1948: 109–10) and repeated by Wilbert (1962), seems very personal; never did I hear it formulated or confirmed.

5. A Vanishing Civilization?

1. The process was slow or at least very erratic, if we are to believe old Guajiros today who assert that a number of those living in the mountainous inland regions of the peninsula (Jala'ala, Kusina, and so on) were not familiar with stock breeding in their parents' time. Be that as it may, one fundamental question still cannot be answered satisfactorily in the absence of sufficiently precise information or observation. Why did certain Guajiros so rapidly adopt this new technique? Was this a logical consequence of their mode of political organization, which had established a permanent rivalry between the clans at that time? Did the arrival of the Conquistadors coincide with sudden economic difficulties that might have been due to a variety of causes—recent arrival of the Guajiro in that territory, pushed back by the Caribs, rapid population growth—although some chroniclers claim that domestic animals long remained mere sources of prestige before assuming fundamental importance in the diet and economic exchanges of the Guajiro?

2. A very mobile, unidentified, black or yellowish insect, called *cigarron* in Venezuelan Spanish; probably belongs to the order Hymenoptera

(*Bombus* sp. [?] or *Xylocopa* sp. [?], according to Hildebrandt [1963]).

3. As is made clear by another version. But for the Guajiro the horse is the domestic animal possessing the greatest value as well as the greatest prestige. It is the emblem of wealth; the poor (*wayu majusü*) do not own horses. They serve essentially as a means of transport, but the possession of many of them is a mark of high social rank and they have considerable exchange value, particularly in the payment of the bride price, *pa'üna*.

Horses used to be exhibited on the occasion of all gatherings and festivities (*mi'ira*) at which the "horse race" (*awachira ama*) could be the main event. This took the form of competition in which the young riders were divided into two groups, each "led" by a "narrator" who would sing the praises of each of the horses and riders in his group before the rivals bounded forward, two by two, along a "racecourse" several hundred meters long. But horses have now become rare and these races have almost died out, on account, say the Guajiro, of the great droughts that have decimated the herds. In fact, other economic factors bound up with growing acculturation, including the use of trucks, have hastened their disappearance.

4. This is why a cow was able to guide the "Guajiro Orpheus" to Juya's domain. It is also as "cultivated products," on the side of Juya, that domestic animals are the victims designated by Pulowi, pierced by the arrows of Hunger, her intermediary, during the dry season (lines 6025–6036). For according to some Guajiros wild animals "do not suffer from the drought."

5. It could also be shown that most of the differences between the first and the second tale, dictated by the new message that the latter was intended to express, reveal a "weakening" of the fundamental system of oppositions associated with Juya and Pulowi. Thus it may be assumed that if the action takes place underground, this is just as much to bring out the fact that Sun is not a pure "*juya* principle" as it is to find a reasonable means of making the horses disappear (under the ground rather than in the sky!). Similarly, by sacrificing a woman rather than a man to Pulowi, the myth indirectly conveys the idea that she is a "weakened" Pulowi!

6. Partly because the Guajiro were fierce warriors but also because the peninsula of Guajira, barren and unalluring to the Spaniards, was not worth making any great effort to conquer it.

7. At Castilletes, Cojoro, Paraguaipoa (in Venezuela); at Maicao, Uribia, Riohacha, and so on (in Colombia).

8. *Boletín Indigenista Venezolano*, Año IX, 1–4 (Caracas, 1964), 143. This journal is the official mouthpiece of the Comisión Indigenista, the office of Indian affairs attached at that time to the Ministry of Justice.

Bibliography

ARMSTRONG, JOHN M., and ALFRED MÉTRAUX
1948 "The Goajiro." In *Handbook of South American Indians*, edited by Julian H. Steward, vol. 4. Bureau of American Ethnology Bulletin 143. Washington, D.C.: Smithsonian Institution.

BARRANQUILLA, R.P. JOSÉ AUGUSTÍN
1946 *Así es la Guajira*. Barranquilla: Imprenta Nacional. (2d ed., 1953.)

BOLINDER, GUSTAF
1957 *Indians on Horseback*. London.

CANDELIER, H.
1893 *Rio-Hacha et les Indiens goajires*. Paris.

CASTELLANOS, JUAN DE
1874 *Elegías de varones ilustres de Indias*. 3d ed. Madrid: Biblioteca de Autores Españoles, vol. 4. (1st ed., 1589.)

CAUDMONT, JEAN
1953 "Cuentos y leyendas de la Guajira." *Revista Colombiana de Folklore*, no. 2. Bogotá.

CELEDÓN, RAFAEL, AND E. URICOECHEA
1878 *Gramática, catecismo i vocabulario de la lengua goajira*. Paris: Maisonneuve.

CHAVES, MILCIADES
1946 "Mitos, leyendas y cuentos de la Guajira." *Boletín de Arqueología* 2:305-332. Bogotá.
1953 "La Guajira: Una región y una cultura de Colombia." *Revista Colombiana de Antropología* 1:123-195. Bogotá.

ERNST, ADOLF
1887 "Die ethnographische Stellung der Goajiro-Indianer." *Zeitschrift für Ethnologie* 19:425-444.
1959 "La posición etnográfica de los indios guajiros." *Boletín Indigenista Venezolano* 7:45-69. (Translated from Ernst 1887.)

FUCHS, H.
1960 "Totemismus und Sozialstruktur der Guajiro." In *Akten der 34 Internationalen Amerikanisten Kongressen*, pp. 585-591. Vienna.

GUHL, E., V. GUTIÉRREZ, R. PINEDA, A. J. STAFFE, ET AL.
1963 *Indios y blancos en la Goajira*, edited by R.P. Lino. Bogotá: Tercer Mundo.

GUTIÉRREZ DE PINEDA, VIRGINIA
1948 "Organización social en la Guajira." *Revista del Instituto Etnológico Nacional*, vol. 3, Bogotá. 267 pp.

HERNÁNDEZ DE ALBA, GREGORIO

1935   "Historia y etnología de las tribus guajiras." *Boletín de Historia y Antigüedades* 23(257) :9–44. Bogotá.

HILDEBRANDT, MARTA

1963   *Diccionario guajiro-español*. Lenguas indígenas de Venezuela, vol. 2. Caracas: Publicación de la Comisión Indigenista.

ISAACS, J.

1884   "Estudio de la lengua guajira." *Anales de la Instrucción Pública en los Estados Unidos de Colombia*, no. 45:216–241. Bogotá.

IZQUIERDO, M.

1956   In *Mitología Americana*. Bogotá.

JAHN, ALFREDO

1927   *Los aborígenes del Occidente de Venezuela*. Caracas. (Reprint, Caracas: Monte Avila, 1973.)

LÉVI-STRAUSS, CLAUDE

1962   *La Pensée sauvage*. Paris: Plon. (Translated as *The Savage Mind*, Chicago: University of Chicago Press, 1968.)

1964   *Mythologiques I: Le Cru et le cuit*. Paris: Plon. (Translated as *The Raw and the Cooked*, New York: Harper & Row, 1969.)

1967   *Mythologiques II: Du miel aux cendres*. Paris: Plon. (Translated as *From Honey to Ashes*, Chicago: University of Chicago Press, 1973.)

1968   *Mythologiques III: L'Origine des manières de table*. Paris: Plon. (Translated as *The Origin of Table Manners*, New York: Harper & Row, 1979.)

1971   *Mythologiques IV: L'Homme nu*. Paris: Plon. (Translated as *The Naked Man*, New York: Jonathan Cape and Harper & Row, 1981.)

LÓPEZ, ANTONIO J.

1957   *Las dolores de una raza*. Maracaibo.

MÉTRAUX, ALFRED

1949   "Religion and Shamanism." In *Handbook of South American Indians*, vol. 5. Washington, D.C.: Smithsonian Institution.

MÚGICA, R.P. CAMILO DE TORRANO

1952   *Guía guajira*. Riohacha, Colombia.

1969   *Aprenda el guajiro: Gramática y vocabularios*. Riohacha: Vicario Apostólico.

PAZ, RAMÓN

1973   *Mitos, leyendas y cuentos guajiros*. Caracas: Instituto Agrario Nacional.

PERRIN, MICHEL

1970   "Introducción a la literatura oral de los indios guajiros." *Economía y Ciencias Sociales*, no. 3:5–20. Caracas.

1971   "La Littérature orale des Guajiro: Compte rendu de mission." *L'Homme* 11(2) :109–112.

1973   "Contribution à l'étude de la littérature orale des Indiens goajiro." Thèse de Troisième Cycle, E.P.H.E., Paris. Mimeographed.

1975   "Mythes et rêves, rituel et chamanisme chez les Indiens guajiro:

Compte rendu de mission." *L'Homme* 15 (2) : 109–113.

PINEDA, ROBERTO
1947   "La Chama, un mito guajiro." *Revista de Folklore,* no. 2 : 113–126. Bogotá.
1950   "Aspectos de la magía en la Guajira." *Revista del Instituto Etnológico Nacional* 3 (1) : 1–164. Bogotá.

POLANCO, JOSÉ ANTONIO
1954   "Noticias guajiras por un guajiro: El Aútshi o Piache guajiro." *Boletín Indigenista Venezolano* 2 : 55–60. Caracas.
1958a "Noticias guajiras por un guajiro: Los velorios o 'lloros' (Arapaja y Ayaraja)." *Boletín Indigenista Venezolano* 3–5 : 197–204.
1958b "Noticias guajiras por un guajiro: El blanqueo o majáyüraa." *Boletín Indigenista Venezolano* 6 : 131–136.
1959   "Noticias guajiras por un guajiro: La petición de mano (Schikü Achuntanunaa)." *Boletín Indigenista Venezolano* 7 : 147–150.

RECLUS, ELISÉE
1881   *Voyage à la Sierra-Nevada de Sainte-Marthe.* Paris: Hachette.

SEBAG, LUCIEN
1971   *L'Invention du monde chez les Indiens pueblo.* Paris: Maspero.

SEKELJ, TIBOR
1952   "Pintura facial de la mujer guajira." *Archivos Venezolanos de Folklore* 1 (1) : 156–158. Caracas.

SIMONS, F. A. A.
1885   "An Exploration of the Goajira Peninsula." *Proceedings of the Royal Geographical Society* 7 : 781–796. London.

TURRADO MORENO, ANGEL
1950   *Cómo son los guajiros.* Caracas: Tercera Conferencia Interamericana de Agricultura.

VEGAMIAN, P. FÉLIX MARÍA DE
1955   *Cómo es la Guajira.* Cuadernos Verdes No. 87. Caracas: Tercera Conferencia Interamericana de Agricultura.

WATSON, LAWRENCE CRAIG
1967   "Guajiro Social Structure: A Reexamination." *Antropológica,* no. 20 : 3–36. Caracas.
1968a *Guajiro Personality and Urbanization.* Los Angeles: UCLA Latin American Center.
1968b "The Inheritance of Livestock in Guajiro Society." *Antropológica,* no. 23 : 3–17. Caracas.

WILBERT, JOHANNES
1962   "Literatura oral y creencias de los Indios goajiros." In *Memorias de la Sociedad de Ciencias Naturales La Salle,* pp. 103–115. Caracas.
1970   *Guajiro Kinship and the Eiruku Cycle.* Los Angeles: UCLA Latin American Center. (Reprinted from *Essays in Honor of Ralph Leon Beals.*)

Index

For animals and plants, the scientific name follows the Guajiro name.